THE LEARNING PROCESS

WITHDRAWN

HERBERT GINSBURG
University of Maryland Baltimore County

D. VAN NOSTRAND COMPANY

New York • Cincinnati • Toronto • London • Melbourne

For my parents
and
For my children,
Deborah
Rebecca
and
Jonathan

D. Van Nostrand Company Regional Offices:
New York   Cincinnati

D. Van Nostrand Company International Offices:
London   Toronto   Melbourne

Library of Congress Catalog Card Number 76-47212
ISBN: 0-442-22695-0

Published by D. Van Nostrand Company
450 West 33rd Street, New York, N.Y. 10001
10 9 8 7 6 5 4 3 2

Material on page 30 from Aims of education by Alfred North Whitehead (Copyright 1929 by Macmillan Publishing Co., Inc., renewed 1957 by Evelyn Whitehead).

Material on page 64 from Language of Science by Tobias Dantzig (Copyright 1930, 1933, 1939, 1954 by Macmillan Publishing Co., renewed 1948, 1961, 1967 by Anna G. Dantzig).

Preface

This book has two aims. The first is to show how children learn, do, and understand elementary mathematics, especially arithmetic. The second is to demonstrate how such knowledge can be used to improve mathematics education and to resolve children's difficulties in learning.

To achieve the first aim, I describe how children learn to count, how they perform basic calculations, how their mathematical ideas and intuitions develop, and I explain why they experience difficulty in learning arithmetic. The book brings to light an often unrecognized side of children's nature: it describes not only their school arithmetic but also the mathematical work in which they spontaneously engage at home and on the playground. We shall see that significant mathematics learning takes place outside the school setting. The book examines children closely and emphasizes competencies that usually go unnoticed. To be sure, children often fail at school mathematics. But these same children know and can do a great deal that remains hidden in the school setting. In short, the first aim of the book is psychological. In the spirit of Piaget, I try to show how the child's mind operates and develops as he or she encounters mathematical problems in and out of school.

My conclusions concerning children's arithmetic are based on over five years of original observations and interviews by myself and colleagues, as well as on the information available in the published literature. Many of the original observations concern my own three children. Other observations involve children in America, England, and Ivory Coast, West Africa. My approach almost never involves standard tests and is seldom concerned with the routine array of

iii

Piagetian problems. I do not stress the standard Piagetian experiments since they have only limited relevance for our concerns. Instead, my observations focus on children counting pennies at home, on African children learning to do a "practical arithmetic" in the marketplace, or on school children trying to solve elementary arithmetic problems. The primary method is the in-depth interview with children as they are in the process of grappling with various sorts of problems. The main concern is not so much with right or wrong answers as with how children go about getting them and what they think about them. Interviews like these, involving close observation of individuals, are rare in mathematics education but essential to improving it.*

The second aim of the book is to show how knowledge of children's mathematics can be used to help them learn. I try to accomplish this aim in several ways. The main one is to present some general insights and principles that can organize and direct helping efforts, both in the classroom and the home. For example, one principle is based on the observation that much of young children's spontaneous arithmetic, developed in their natural environment, involves counting, especially with the fingers. Since this is so, early education in mathematics should place a major emphasis on counting as a basis for arithmetic.

In addition to presenting general principles of this type, I make a few specific suggestions concerning teaching practices. But my main aim is not to offer specific curricula or teaching methods. Many different ways of implementing the principles are both possible and desirable; no one curriculum or approach will solve all problems of mathematics education. As William James said many years ago:

> You make a great, a very great mistake, if you think that psychology, being the science of the mind's laws, is something from which you can deduce definite programmes and schemes and methods of instruction for immediate schoolroom use. Psychology is a science, and teaching is an art; and sciences never generate arts directly out of themselves. An intermediary inventive mind must make the application, by using its originality.[1]

---

*A note on how observations are identified in the text. Those concerning Deborah, Rebecca, and Jonathan involve the writer's children. Almost all are derived from video tape recordings and hence are extremely accurate. Other observations identified only by the child's first name have been gathered by the writer or his colleague, Dr. Ezra Heitowit. The vast majority of these, too, are derived from videotape recordings. Observations borrowed from other writers are identified both by the child's first name and the writer's last (e.g., Renwick's Moira), and an appropriate reference is given.

I believe that the book can be valuable to those who are concerned with young children's mathematics. The book requires no technical background in either mathematics or psychology. It should be of use to parents and teachers who want to help children learn arithmetic in or out of school. It should be useful to special education professionals, school psychologists, and social workers who are interested in obtaining a new perspective on learning difficulties and even disabilities. Mathematics educators may want to read the book to acquire deeper insight into the targets of their curricula—the children. Developmental psychologists may find the book to be a useful example of how their discipline can be applied to real educational problems. Clinical psychologists may find the approach described in this book helpful in dealing with children's intellectual difficulties.

Part I begins with an account of the largely spontaneous development of counting and elementary arithmetic in children from birth to about 6 or 7 years of age. Each chapter treats a different aspect of learning, and in most chapters there are "boxes" containing material that is not central to the argument but which the reader may find of some interest. The main purpose of Part I is to show how elementary competence in arithmetic develops in virtually all children throughout the world. This competence is a kind of informal "intuition" that can be used as a sound basis for formal instruction in mathematics.

Part II focuses on the written mathematics taught in school. The main aim is to show that children's school mathematics is not always what it seems. Children solve problems in unusual ways of which teachers and tests are often unaware. And children—virtually all of them—possess important competencies which are sometimes ignored or suppressed in the process of teaching. I show how these can be used to produce dramatic gains in achievement and understanding.

It is a pleasure to acknowledge many different kinds of help that made this book possible. The College of Human Ecology and the Center for Research in Education, both at Cornell University, and the National Science Foundation provided financial support for the project. Some of the research was undertaken in collaboration with Robert Davis, who in many ways inspired and supported the project. Ezra Heitowit was invaluable as Research Associate, interviewing many children. My students were a constant source of stimulation and criticism: Barbara Allardice, Arthur Baroody, Lynn De Jonghe,

Kathy Hebbeler, Mary Kennedy, Greg Lehne, Anita Levy, David Littman, Jane Megaw, Andrea Petitto, Jill Posner, Bob Russell, Marilyn Samuels, Liz Spelke. Several individuals were kind enough to comment on various versions of the manuscript: Barbara Allardice, Robert Davis, Kathy Hebbeler, Barbara Koslowski. They made many useful suggestions. Many thanks go to the children, particularly in Ithaca, who were willing to talk with us, and to the school officials, particularly Lillian Tuskey, at Henry St. John School, who gave us a pleasant and encouraging atmosphere in which to work. The government of the Ivory Coast, the chiefs of the villages, and the traders in the market place have been most generous with their hospitality. The Ivorian observations were largely collected by Jill Posner in connection with her thesis. The best typist in the world is clearly Elizabeth Swartwout and a close second is Sandy Rightmyer. They contributed above and beyond the call of duty. Finally, a very special debt to my wife and best critic, Jane Knitzer, who always supported me in this work, clarified my thinking, and encouraged the next step. Many thanks.

Contents

PART ONE: INFORMAL ARITHMETIC   1

1. LEARNING TO COUNT   3

Number Words: A Song to Sing   3
Summary   9
Principles   9
Things: How Many Are There?   10
Summary   19
Principles   20
Ideas: What Does "Five" Mean?   21
Summary   28
Principles   29

2. CONCEPTS IN BABIES AND LITTLE CHILDREN   30

Baby Mathematics   30
The Young Child   33
Summary   41
Principles   42

3. LEARNING PRACTICAL ARITHMETIC   44

Learning: Why and How   44
Summary   51

Principles   52
Practical Arithmetic   52
Summary   65
Principles   66

4. HELPING YOUNG CHILDREN   67

PART TWO: SCHOOL LEARNING   77

5. COMPUTING WITH WRITTEN NUMBERS   79

Writing and Reading   79
Understanding   84
Summary   89
Principles   90
Computing: The Child's Secret Inventions   90
Summary   105
Principles   106

6. MISTAKES   107

The Nature and Origins of Mistakes   107
Patterns of Success and Failure   116
Gaps   121
Summary   128
Principles   129

7. LEARNING DIFFICULTIES   130

Bob and George   131
Patty   136
Stacy   144

8. UNDERSTANDING   150

Connecting   150

Summary 159
Principles 159
Perceiving 160
Summary 168
Principle 168

9. TESTING AND TEACHING 169

END NOTES **185**

REFERENCES **191**

INDEX **195**

Informal Arithmetic

Psychology has recently made surprising discoveries concerning the intellectual development of preschool children. Infants perceive the world in sophisticated ways and display planned and purposeful behavior. Toddlers accomplish truly impressive feats of learning when they master early grammar and meaning. By 4 or 5, children's intellectual interests are wide-ranging: they have notions of time, space, and causality. The growth of mind from birth to five or six years of age is truly spectacular.

One part of these great accomplishments involves "informal" mathematics. Before entrance to school, children develop a beginning understanding of number—they count, they construct elementary concepts, and they learn to put counting and concepts together to solve real problems. In the first few years of school, children continue to develop their own informal arithmetic. Part I focuses on these developments from infancy through age 7 or 8.

Chapter 1

Learning to Count

For several years young children struggle with counting. They learn the number words; they apply them to things; and they try to understand what counting is all about.

NUMBER WORDS: A SONG TO SING

Memorizing "one," "two," "three" . . .

Number words fill the world of young children. They hear "one, two, three . . ." on television and in stories. Three- or four-year olds shout the number words in games and sing them in songs. Adults say "one, two, three . . ." as they point to things, as they remove cans from the shelf in the store, and as they use a pencil to make marks on a piece of paper.

Children try to say these words themselves but experience considerable difficulty. One problem is that there seem to be an awful lot of the "one, two, three . . ." words. If you learn to say "one, two, three . . ." and think that you are finished, someone will always come along and say "four, five, six . . ."; and if you learn "four, five, six," someone will say "seven, eight, nine." The end is never in sight.

Also, people are very fussy about how you say these words. You have to say "four, five, six"; you cannot say "four, six, five." Children become confused: what's wrong with "four, six, five?" Aren't they exactly the same words as "four, five, six?"

So young children are faced with two important problems with respect to the counting words: there are a lot to learn; and they must be said in certain ways and not others.

They solve the first problem—the apparently endless number of number words—by limiting what they try to learn at any one time. They struggle with "one" through "five" before they try "six" through "ten." They carefully regulate their own learning and attempt only a little more than they can master at one time.

The second problem is harder. Why is it wrong to say "one, three, two" but right to say "one, two, three?" Gradually, children resolve this difficulty too. They begin to see a pattern in the apparent chaos of number words. They perceive that numbers are like a song: the number words involve a sequence of sounds *in the same order all the time.* Young children make a great discovery when they learn that "two" always comes after "one" and "three" always after "two." Numbers are not so mysterious after all. They are a song to sing in which you must remember not only the words but also their right order.

The problem therefore becomes one of learning a song with a particular ordering of words. In the song, "six" always comes after "five" and never after "ten" at the end of the song (or what seems like the end). It is now clear that order is important, but it is not obvious how you can remember it. Is there any clue that tells you what comes next? Is there any way of knowing that "seven" comes after "six" and not after "nine?" Young children try to make sense out of their world, but they can find no order in the song. The "one, two, three . . . " song is just like other meaningless songs which offer no way of predicting the order of sounds. (Remember "tizovthee" as in "My country tizovthee?") Consequently, they have little choice but to memorize the song by rote.

With practice, children learn the sequence of number words slowly and with some difficulty. Their parents try to make the task simpler by imposing on it some rhyme (if not reason): "one, two, buckle my shoe; three, four, close the door . . ." This is intended as a device to reduce the load on brute memory and thereby make the numbers easier to learn. Still, children have a lot to memorize and it is not until they are three or four years old that they learn to say the beginning numbers.[1] Of course, there are many individual differences in children's counting; some children count higher and some lower. But eventually almost all children learn the small numbers.

Once the song is learned, children are asked to sing it in some strange ways: say what comes after "three"; skip every other word ("two, four, six . . ."); sing it backwards ("ten, nine, eight . . ."); and so on. We can ourselves get some appreciation for the difficulty this causes young children by performing a little experiment on our knowledge of *Jack and Jill.* "Let us ask a friend to test us in this fashion: what word comes before *down?* What word comes after *his?*

Go through the verse saying only every second word. Say only every third word. Say the whole verse backward."² The task is quite hard, and it is the same kind of task children have to do with "one, two, three. . . ."

Learning bigger numbers

After laboriously memorizing the first part of the song—"one" to about "twelve"—young children encounter a welcome surprise. They discover that the second part—"fourteen" onward—is considerably easier to learn. Indeed, doing the second part requires very little brute memory. All they need to learn are a few simple rules.

To see how this can be so, consider Rebecca's learning some big numbers. At four years and eleven months (4–11), she and her identical twin sister, Deborah, were sitting at the table, eating lunch, and engaged in the following conversation.

Deborah (D): 1, 2, 1, 2, 1, 2.

Rebecca (R): 1, 2, 3.

D: No, not like that. I said, 1, 2, 1, 2, 1, 2.

R: 1, 2, 3, 4, 5, 6, 7, 8.

D: 1, 2, 3, 4, 5, 6, 7, 8, 9, 10, 11, 12, 13, 14, 15, 16, 17, 18, 19.

Rebecca then asked her mother, "What's after 19?" Rebecca knew that there were numbers beyond 19 because she had been exposed to them before. This was not the first time she had asked such a question.

Mother (M): 20.

R: 20, 21, 22, 23, 24, 25, 26, 27, 28, 29. What's after?

Notice that Rebecca needed only one number—the 20—in order to construct a whole string of numbers, at least up to 29.

M: 30.

R: 31, 32, 33, 34, 35, 36, 37, 38, 39. Now 40.

M: Good.

R: 41, 42, 43, 44, 45, 46, 47, 48, 49. [Pause] 50.

M: Good.

R: 51, 52, 53, 54, 55, 56, 57, 58, 59.

Here Rebecca paused and looked at her mother, apparently in search of the next number.

M: 60.

This observation makes it clear that Rebecca was no longer engaged in the rote memorization of some meaningless sounds. Instead, she was learning some basic patterns in the number song; she was discovering rules. One important rule that she acquired was that after a tens number—20, 30, 40—you can simply add on the numbers from 1 to 9. If you can say "forty," then you just continue by saying, "forty-one, forty-two . . ." until you reach "forty-nine."

How can we tell that a rule governs Rebecca's behavior and that she did not merely memorize? One bit of evidence is that she did not ask, "What comes after forty?" Given 40 or 30, she could rattle off the rest of the sequence with ease, and got stuck again only when she reached the next tens number. Also, if she were engaged in memorizing, she would find 40 easier to memorize than 41 (since the latter is longer when you say it), but clearly she did not. And the final proof is that some children make the mistake of saying "twenty-eight, twenty-nine, twenty-ten" or "thirty-nine, thirty-ten." Such a mistake could only be the product of a rule; the child has never heard "twenty-ten" or "thirty-ten" and so could not possibly have memorized it.

Rebecca was also engaged in learning a second rule, as the continuation of the episode shows.

Soon the girls returned to counting.

R: 20, 21, 22, 23, 24, 25, 26, 27, 28.

M: You do an awful lot of counting.

R: 15, 16, 17. What's after 21?

M: 22.

R: 22, 23, 24, 25, 26, 27, 28, 29.

At this point she indicated by a glance that she wanted her mother to supply the next number.

M: 30.

R: 40, 50, 60, 70, 80, 90, tenny.

Rebecca was making an attempt to discover a rule for constructing the tens (10, 20, etc.). One piece of evidence is that she counted by tens. Why tens unless she was concerned with learning them? Another is the word "tenny"; it had not been taught her, nor had she ever heard it on television or seen it in books. "Tenny" was her own invention. And she did not decide on "tenny" through some kind of random process. The word resulted instead from her seeing a pattern in the numbers: in general, each tens word *does* have *-ty* at the end of it. To get the tens numbers, all you have to do is add *-ty* to the number words from "two" to "ten" and then just change them a little. "Two-ty" and "three-ty" need a bit of changing to get "twenty" and "thirty," but "four-ty," "six-ty," "seven-ty," "eight-ty," and "nine-ty" are easier and more straightforward. Using this rule, you get as the natural outcome "tenny" or "tenty." Of course, Rebecca could not verbalize the rule and was probably not even aware of it. Nevertheless, a rule does seem to have been the force behind her behavior.

Rebecca is not the only child who learns counting in this way. At four years of age, Court's Paul was intensely interested in counting and was obviously engaged in picking up the rules.[3] For example, he asked what comes after 100; his mother said, 101; and that information was enough to convey a rule which enabled him to count to 199. At 5-1, Paul tried to learn counting by fives and by himself managed to do 5, 10, 15, 20. His mother supplied 25 and he did 30.

Court relates the following episode: "Seeing that he stopped, I supplied 35 and he said '35, 40.' I again supplied 45, and he said '45, 50, 55, 60' and stopped. 65 was again my contribution and he said, '65, 70, 75, 80, 85, 90, 95, 100. Heee . . . I can count that way, to 100! Is that by fives?' . . . I do not know why he suddenly began to count by fives. But . . . I heard him count by fives up to two hundred."[4] Like Rebecca, Paul had figured out a rule for counting and used it to generate new numbers.

Similarly, other children make mistakes like Rebecca's. Asked to count backwards, Grossman's John said, "Eighteen, seventeen, sixteen, fi— fifteen, I was about to say fiveteen."[5] Drummond's Margaret said, "Is there a fifteen?" as well as "forty-nine, forty-ten, forty-eleven, forty-twelve."[6] And Court's Paul enjoyed the joke of saying "tenty, eleventy, twelvty."[7] In exactly the same way, unschooled children in Ivory Coast, West Africa, among the Baoulé and Dioula tribes, say numbers like "ten-ten" for 20, "twenty-ten" for 30, and so on.[8] Children everywhere seem to construct the number words by rule!

Mistakes in Early Speech

Young children's errors of speech are quite similar to their counting errors. One example of speech errors that every parent encounters involves the four-year-old who says, "I *goed* to the store" or "He *bringed* the book." Psychologists who have investigated early language point out that mistakes of this type teach us several interesting things. First, children's language is based on rules. Children never hear "goed" or "bringed" and hence cannot just be mimicking use of these words. Instead, the words must be the product of a rule to the effect that past tense is indicated by adding "-ed" to the stem. Of course children are not aware of this rule, just as adult speakers are not aware of many language rules. Nevertheless, rules govern speech.

Second, children's rules are derived in sensible ways from their experience. Children have frequently heard "-ed" used quite correctly to indicate past tense—for example, "helped" or "waited." So their rule is a sensible one, based on real experience. It is not a figment of their imagination. The main mistake children make is in applying it too widely—to all verbs. They need to learn the exceptions, like "went" and "brought," so that they can avoid overgeneralization. *Children's mistakes frequently have a rational basis.*

Third, the mistakes children make are the result of a search for meaning. In learning a language, children do not aim merely to imitate what they have heard. Instead, they look for underlying structure, for what is really going on. They do not simply repeat strings of words; they try instead to construct rules at a deeper level. Sometimes they are wrong, but their mistakes indicate that they are digging below the surface.

As we shall see, the same holds true in children's mathematics. Their counting mistakes result from an overgeneralized application of rules; the rules reflect children's experiences; and they are constructed as the result of an attempt to understand. In language as in number, children's intellectual learning is in part a creative, intelligent process. Rote, "mechanical" factors play a secondary role.

There is not much difference in older children's learning of number words. Common observation shows that at least until adolescence they continue to memorize a few words ("thousand," "million," "billion") and learn more rules to produce bigger numbers (for example, how to get numbers after a billion). All this is relatively easy. The hardest task has already been accomplished by the four-year-old who discovered that the song makes some sense.

SUMMARY

Trying to learn the number words that they frequently hear, young children encounter several difficulties. The string of number words seems to be endless (and it *is!*). Also, although they must be said in exactly the right way, what constitutes the right way is not clear. Children cope with the first problem by limiting what they try to learn at any one time. Concentrating on the first several numbers, they make an important discovery; the right way to say the number words involves a certain sequence of sounds in the same order all the time. Unfortunately, the beginning of the sequence—the first twelve or so numbers—is completely arbitrary. There is no rational basis for predicting what comes after a certain number. Therefore, children have to memorize the smaller numbers in a rote fashion. After a period of time, they discover that the numbers after about 13 contain an underlying pattern. Using it, children develop a few simple rules by which to generate the numbers up to about 100.

PRINCIPLES

It is now possible to propose a few general principles.

1. *Children search for meaning.* Children try to make sense of the world by looking for an underlying pattern, for a deeper meaning. Sometimes it does not exist, as in the case of the first twelve or so numbers. But often it does: the larger numbers display clear underlying regularities. Having searched these out, children use them to develop rules for producing the larger numbers themselves. The exploitation of underlying patterns makes intellectual work easier and more efficient, and allows children to avoid the drudgery of rote memorization.

2. *Errors are meaningful and informative.* Children's errors are seldom, if ever, random or meaningless. Most often they provide insight into what children are really trying to do. Thus, they say "twenty-ten" because they are trying to capture the underlying structure of the counting numbers, not because they weren't thinking.

3. *Children can use different learning strategies depending on environmental circumstances.* When there is no underlying pattern to the numbers, children memorize them in a rote fashion. When the pattern is there to be found, they exploit it. Some learning is done by rote, some is meaningful. Children do not learn in only one way.

4. *Children can learn in apparently adverse circumstances.*

Children learn a great deal about numbers outside of school, without instruction or special help; indeed their parents are often unaware that they are trying to learn numbers. Also, they manage to learn even though their experience is often chaotic and confusing, not to say unplanned. For example, children may hear adults counting by twos or by fives before they have mastered counting by ones. Nevertheless, they manage to learn.

THINGS: HOW MANY ARE THERE?

Children have seen that the number words follow one another in strict order. And they have learned to say many of them. Next they have to learn how these words are applied to things.

In their natural environment, children sometimes see their parents pointing to things as they say the number words. They poke a finger at a block and say "one"; at another block and say "two"; and on it goes. Sometimes there is no pointing, as when their parents take them up the stairs and say "one, two, three . . ." until they get to the top. Every day, the same words on the same stairs, and "fifteen" is always the last one. In other situations there is sometimes very rapid pointing and a funny kind of counting: their parents dash through a large collection of pennies, saying "two, four, six. . . ."

These experiences confuse children. They do not know what numbers to say in connection with a group of things. If you just say "one, two, three . . ." to as high a number as you know, you are apt to be wrong. What's the secret then? It may be important to poke your finger at things. How should that be done? But since parents do not always do it, should it be done at all, and if so, when?

For several years, then, young children engage in the pleasant struggle of learning to attach the numbers they can already say to the objects they can see. They begin by learning to count small numbers of objects. Then they must repeat the learning process with larger numbers. Counting must be conquered and reconquered, as children encounter larger and larger numbers of things.

Early mistakes in counting things

Initially, the way children count things is inconsistent. The first time they count, they get one answer; the next time, another. They do not know which answer is right, or may even think that both are.

At 4–6, Samantha was presented with a collection of candies randomly arranged on a table, as in Figure 1–1. Her job was to count the candies. A very precocious girl, she had no difficulty in saying

Figure 1–1. *A random array of candies*

the number words; indeed, she could easily reach 100. Yet in counting the candies, she made many errors. On one try, she would get 23; on another, 24; on yet another, 22. Which was right? She had no idea. Her procedure was to point to each candy in its original location; she did not bother to push any candies aside after counting them. Because of this, she forgot which were counted and which were not. She counted several candies twice and several not at all, and as a result got different results each time. This inconsistency did not disturb her in the slightest. So children sometimes believe that the same collection can be characterized by two or more numbers.

Another example of this kind of error involves Deborah and Rebecca. At 4–11, they were engaged in counting the numbers of fingers on a hand. Like most children, they enjoyed counting for its own sake and frequently did it. Rebecca showed Deborah three fingers and asked, "Know how many this is?" Deborah counted one by one to get the correct result. But then each child tried to count the fingers of both hands together. Rebecca counted hers and claimed, "I've got ten fingers."

Deborah disagreed. She counted her own (ten) fingers and got 16. Like Samantha, Deborah believed that two identical collections (the twins' ten fingers) could have different numbers (10 and 16).

Rebecca said, "We don't get 16. Want me to count your fingers?" She then counted Deborah's fingers and got 10.

Deborah counted both hands and again got the wrong result. Next she counted the fingers on one hand and got 6.

Rebecca counted the same fingers and got 5. Rebecca showed Deborah what 6 really is—namely, 5 on one hand and 1 on the other.

Deborah held up the fingers of one hand and insisted, "This is 6 too; this is 6 too!" Deborah believed that two different collections (her five fingers and Rebecca's six) could both be characterized by the same number 6.

Determining a set's number is a formidable task for young children. Perhaps the most frequent difficulty is the tendency to get different results on repeated countings of the same set. First children get 10; then they carefully count again and get 11. Not only is their counting unreliable; they also see nothing wrong in it! There is no contradiction in counting ten fingers one time, and eleven the next.

Why counting is hard

Why should counting cause so much trouble? Clearly the problem is not the result of faulty language. Deborah knew the number of words up to about 20, but could not correctly count six things. Typically, children can *say* the number words quite well up to a reasonable limit but cannot *count* a set of things whose number is well below that limit. At least in the case of counting, adequate language does not guarantee accurate results. Children need to learn more than words alone.

If language is not the problem, what is? To count properly, children must know how to do *at least* the following:

1. To say the number words in their proper order. We have already seen that children can more easily do this than count things.

2. To count each member of the relevant collection once and only once. That is, children must not count one object two times or forget to count an object.

3. To make a one-to-one correspondence between each number word and each thing. The word "one" has to go with this object and "two" with that object. "One" cannot go with both. Each object must be assigned one and only one number word.

At least three skills are needed for accurate counting of things: saying the number words, considering each thing once, and one-to-one correspondence. The first of these presents no obstacle; difficulty with the second and third prevents children from counting well.

Suppose that children are given a task that requires them to consider things once and only once.[9] Shown a page of pictures, as in Figure 1–2, children are told to touch each thing "just once" or

Figure 1–2. *Some forms to touch*

"only once." They do not have to count, just touch. In this situation young children (from 2–7 to 4–3) find it difficult to indicate things once and only once. Their dominant error is pointing to the same thing twice. A lesser error is forgetting to point to a picture at all. Naturally, these mistakes are more frequent in younger children within this age range; but virtually all preschool children make errors of this type.

Why are there so many errors on a task that to us *seems* trivially easy? One reason is that young children seem to forget which items have been touched and which have not. They lack a systematic plan for making sure that each picture has been considered once and only once. Using a haphazard procedure, they touch the circle first, then the triangle, then the trapezoid, and so on. Doing this puts a great strain on children's memories; to be correct, they must remember the characteristics of each individual item touched. For example, on the fourth choice, they must remember that they have already touched the circle, triangle, and trapezoid. Since there is so much to keep in mind at the same time, they frequently forget and therefore count some things twice and some not at all. Young children are not very methodical or organized. They do not make is easy for themselves to consider things once and only once.*

Children also have trouble with one-to-one correspondence. Piaget, the famous Swiss psychologist, some of whose ideas we will encounter several times in this book, presented young children with the following task involving one-to-one correspondence.[10] He showed individual children six little bottles and a larger number of glasses on a tray. Piaget asked the children to "take off the tray just enough glasses, the same number as there are bottles, one for each bottle." (Similar problems involved eggs and egg cups, and flowers and vases.) The children (around four to five years of age) produced† arrangements like that in Figure 1–3. Instead of putting out one glass for each bottle, they made a line of glasses that was the same

---

*Psychologists have recently documented many instances of the lack of planning in young children. For example, they neglect to organize material for memory and hence exhibit poor recall. Given a list of things to remember—ball, cat, carrot, bat, dog, tomato, and so on—they fail to group similar things together (ball, bat; cat, dog; carrot, tomato). Such a strategy would make it easier to remember things. Older children plan such groupings, but younger ones tend not to.

†Piaget is not interested in establishing exact age norms. Instead, he is concerned with the *sequence* of development. He wants to know whether the child goes through Stage I before Stage II and Stage II before Stage III. He is not concerned about the exact ages at which all this occurs, partly because he recognizes that there are wide individual differences due to experience and other factors.

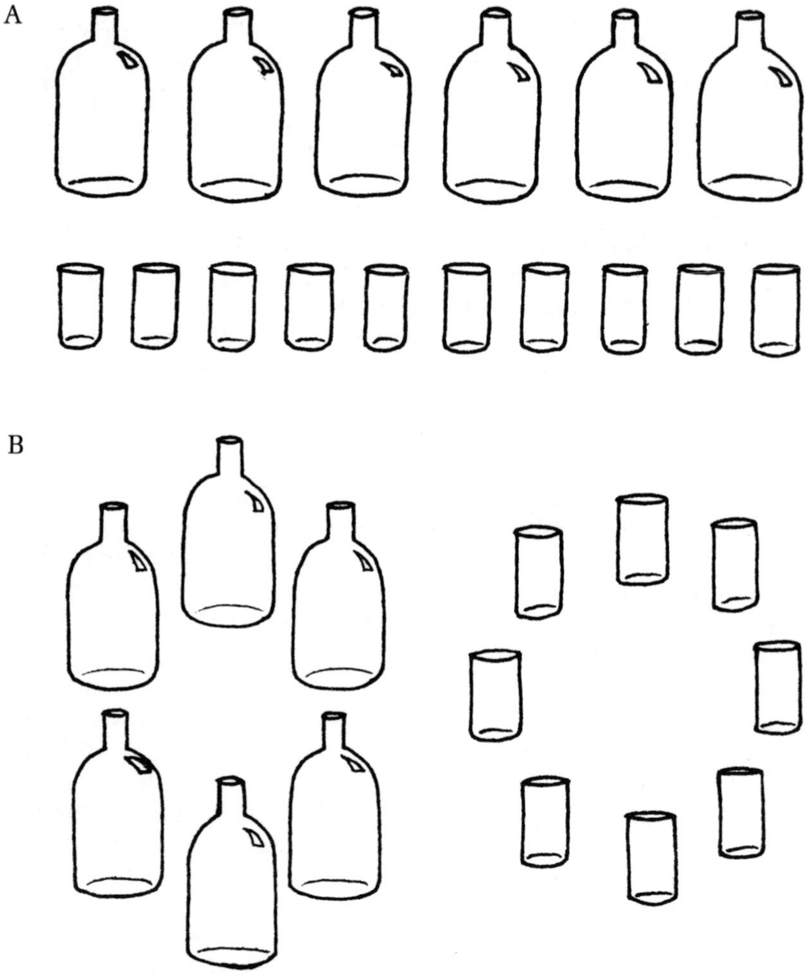

Figure 1–3. *The young child's arrangement of glasses and bottles*

length as the line of bottles, even though both had different numbers of objects (Figure 1–3A). Or, shown six bottles in a circle, they might put out eight glasses, also in a circle (Figure 1–3B). The crucial factor was *appearance*. If the collections *looked* similar (same length or shape), the children thought they had the same number. The children were unable to use one-to-one correspondence: they could not pair each bottle with a glass. Presumably, they also have difficulty in matching spoken numbers with real objects.

In brief, young children's difficulty in counting things is not due to inability to say the counting numbers. Rather, their problem can be traced to specific characteristics of thought: they cannot plan strategies for dealing with things once and only once; and they find it hard to make a one-to-one correspondence between the numbers they say and the things they touch.

Strategies for counting things

The child gradually changes these thought patterns and learns to count objects more accurately. The average four-year-old can

---

Can Animals Count?

There have been several accounts of animal mathematicians.[11]

The suspicious crow

A man was determined to shoot a crow which had been making a nuisance of itself. But the crow was both suspicious and clever: it always fled when the man entered the watch house in the field. The man attempted a stratagem to deceive the crow. He sent *two* men to the watch house; after a period of time, one left while the other remained. Did this fool the crow? No, it stayed away.

The next day the man increased the difficulty of the problem. Three man entered the house, and later two left it. But this ploy did not outsmart the crow either. It was therefore necessary for the man to increase the numbers again. Four entered and three left. Still the crow was not deceived. Five entered and four left. Again no result. Success was achieved only when the ante was raised one step further—six entered the house and five left it. Now the crow returned and the remaining man shot it, an action which perhaps leaves something to be desired from the point of view of mathematics education.

Lonely Boston Brahmins

The insect world furnishes further examples of animal mathematics. The solitary wasps supply to their young, living in different cells of the nest, a certain number of victims. One species consistently feeds its young a meal of one large caterpillar. Another species always provides its dependents with a dinner of five victims; another with 10; another 14; and another 24. There is thus a characteristic number that each species habitually employs. Most remarkably, in one species if the young are male (and hence small), the wasp supplies five victims, whereas if the young are female (and large) the wasp provides 10!

count up to about nine objects without error; the five-year-old, about 20; the six-year-old, about 28.¹² But more interesting than the improvement are the different *methods* children use to find out how many things there are in a collection.

At first, children have to count things one by one, in laborious fashion, to determine a set's number. Recall Deborah and Rebecca's intense effort to establish the number of fingers on a hand; recall too the difficulty they experienced and their disagreement. It often takes many years and considerable practice with larger and larger numbers before children's counting of things one by one becomes smooth and efficient.

Over a period of time, children learn to "see" small numbers directly. Eventually, they do not even need to count *small* collections—"two, three, four, or five"—to know their number. They can *perceive* X X X as "three," just as they can directly convert the letter *b* into the sound "bee." This kind of instant recognition often is achieved after having counted such sets repeatedly and remembering the results.

Sonya, a first grader, gives a charming account of the process. Presented with an array of dots as in Figure 1–4, she was asked to determine their number. She quickly gave the correct response, "nine."

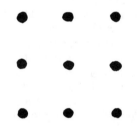

Figure 1–4. *Sonya's array of dots*

Interviewer: How did you find out there were 9?

Sonya: When I was about four years old, I was in nursery school. All I had to do was count. And so, I just go like 1, 2, 3, 4, 5, 6, 7, 8, 9, and I just knew it by heart and I kept on doing it when I was five too. And then I kept knowing 9, you know. Exactly like this [she pointed to the array of nine dots].

In other words, Sonya maintained that in nursery school she had seen many arrays of this type, had counted them, and therefore had established that 3×3 arrays have nine elements. Now she directly perceives 9 in the arrays and no longer needs to count.

So the child's first two methods are counting and immediate recognition. Although tedious, counting works with sets of any size; immediate recognition is effective only for small collections.

Over a period of time, children spontaneously develop grouping strategies which allow them to determine numbers in increasingly efficient ways. Diane, a third grader, was asked to determine the number of the following collection of dots (Figure 1–5).

Figure 1–5. *Diane's array of dots*

Interviewer (I): What do you see inside the box?

Diane (D): Three sets of four rows and one dot here.

I: If you wanted to know how many dots are in the box, how would you find out?

D: Counting by fours. 4, 8, 14, and 1 makes 15.

I: Suppose you wanted to be very certain?

D: 1, 2, 3, . . . 13.

Diane's procedure was intended to yield a valid answer by means of a short cut. Instead of counting one by one, she saw that there were three sets of four elements each; she immediately perceived these naturally existing groupings of elements. Then she used arithmetic (adding or counting by fours and then one) to get the answer. While her arithmetic was faulty, the basic strategy is an extremely economical one, allowing its user to bypass the tedium of counting one by one.

Other children use relatively advanced forms of arithmetic in basically the same strategy. Lori, a third grader, was given the same problem as Diane, and did it this way: "Well, 4 times 3 is 12, plus 1 is 13." Certainly this kind of strategy is easier than counting and if used properly can be just as accurate. So children proceed from counting one by one to applying arithmetic operations to groups of elements.

These sophisticated strategies are extremely widespread and do not seem to depend on schooling. Unschooled tribesmen in Africa show a virtually identical approach to enumeration. Consider the following interview with Fouto, a merchant who sells spare parts for bicycles. He was presented with a problem involving small squares arranged in a pattern quite similar to that shown in Figure 1-5.

Interviewer (I): What could you do to find out how many squares are there . . . the quickest way possible?

Fouto (F): Well, I'd count them of course. If I count to see how many there are in the first line, I can tell you how many there are altogether.

I: Go ahead and count them then.

F: There are 35.

I: How did you come up with that answer?

F: I counted it like this: 1, 2, 3, 4, 5, 6, 7. Then 5 times 7. (This was the same procedure used by Lori.)

Arithmetic in the Unschooled

There are many examples of relatively sophisticated arithmeticlike procedures in unschooled, illiterate individuals. One observation concerns the estimation of number by the Kpelle of Liberia, a tribe of rice farmers, and by Yale undergraduates, a group of youths residing in New Haven, many of whom, like the Kpelle, belong to secret societies.[13] The Kpelle adults and Yale undergraduates were both shown piles of stones, one pile at a time, and were asked to estimate the number, which could vary from 10 to 100, in steps of 10. The statistical results showed that the Kpelle were more accurate at this task than the Yale students. It seems fair to conclude that the Kpelle have sensible techniques for estimating number and that these techniques are effective with familiar objects. Even "primitive" people possess powerful intellectual skills that are adaptive in their environment. It is reassuring to note that given appropriate experience the culturally deprived (from the African point of view) Yale undergraduates managed to catch up with the Kpelle.

How did Fouto learn to multiply?

F: For us, who do not know how to read or write, we merchants have a kind of mental calculation that we do. As soon as you tell me a problem I have to think about it a little and then I can tell you the answer. You learned what you know at school. But we've never been to school. Nevertheless, we have to know how to reckon. We have to know 5 times 5. Every merchant has to know this.

I: Did you ever go to adult night classes?

F: No. I know what I know because I am a merchant by trade.[14]

We see then that in the course of development, individuals become increasingly economical and efficient in their ways of determining the number of a collection. Moreover, this learning is widespread across many cultures and may even take place in the complete absence of schooling.

SUMMARY

Young children spend several years learning how to attach numbers to things. They enjoy counting. At first, their counting is inconsistent. They get one result when they first count a collection and a different result the second time. Such inconsistency does not disturb children. They believe that the *same* set of objects can have at least two *different* numbers; they also believe that two *different* sets can have the *same* number. Learning to count requires more than the ability to say the number words in correct order. Correct counting also requires considering each member of a collection once and only once; and it requires making a one-to-one correspondence between each number word and each thing. The first of these tasks— considering things once and only once—is difficult because young children lack a systematic plan for keeping track of things and hence must rely on rote memory, which soon becomes overburdened. The second task—one-to-one correspondence—is also hard and takes many years to master.

With development, children overcome these difficulties, first with smaller numbers and then with larger ones. They develop several useful strategies for counting. They learn to count one by one with care and accuracy. Perhaps as a result of this, they learn to perceive small numbers directly and no longer need to count them. Then they learn to use arithmetic as a shortcut for counting: they count by twos and add to get a result. Economical procedures like these are widespread across cultures and do not seem to depend on schooling.

PRINCIPLES

1. *The ability to say the numbers does not guarantee their effective application.* Often young children can count out loud very well, reaching numbers as high as 100, but at the same time cannot accurately count a collection of twenty things. Saying the numbers properly is not the same as using them correctly. Too often we tend to equate accurate speech with accurate thought. We think that if children say something well they must understand it. This is not true.

2. *To develop effective counting skills, young children require repetitive experience in the counting of things and can get it in virtually any environment.* In their games, children spend a lot of time counting things over and over again. They enjoy counting. This kind of practice seems necessary to develop effective strategies for considering things once and only once and for perfecting one-to-one correspondence. Children should be able to practice their counting in virtually any normal environment. Pebbles can be as effective as sterilized "educational" blocks.

3. *Young children are engaged in the spontaneous learning of economical strategies for counting things.* As children develop, many of their activities tend towards economy and efficiency. This rule seems to apply to counting. Children develop techniques like repeated addition to make counting easier. This learning may be considered spontaneous for several reasons. Neither parents nor teachers seem to engage in the explicit teaching of these techniques and are usually surprised when a child exhibits them. Indeed, I have encountered many cases (to be discussed more fully in later chapters) in which children failing miserably in school surprised their teachers by utilizing extremely sophisticated techniques for counting objects. Further evidence for spontaneity of learning is provided by the observation that unschooled and illiterate children in African societies employ strategies virtually identical to those used by American children.

4. *Young children must relearn with larger numbers what they already know about smaller ones.* First they may learn to count up to 10 objects one by one; later they must repeat the entire process with larger numbers. First they may learn to enumerate small collec-

tions by addition; later they must learn to apply the same technique to larger numbers. Children's conquests must be repeated at higher and higher levels.

IDEAS: WHAT DOES "FIVE" MEAN?

We have seen that young children learn to say the number words and to determine how many things are in a collection. Asked to count their fingers, they can tell you that there are "five." But what does "five" *mean*? Their "five" may be different from our "five." Do they believe that five fingers are the same as five toys or even five houses? The general issue is this: before schooling begins, how do children conceive of the number words they say or the objects they count?

We shall see that counting and numbers do not have the same meaning for young children as they do for us.

What adults mean by "five"

Suppose that we adults count a collection of objects and determine that it has five elements. For us, "five" is more than just a *word* we say as we point to the last of the objects. Rather, "five" is a *concept* with several related meanings. Indeed, for us, a whole network of knowledge surrounds a cardinal number like "five." This knowledge is very complex, and by no means obvious.

We count the fingers of a hand to get "five." In doing this, we know that:

1. "Five" refers to the collection as a whole. It is a property of all the fingers taken as an aggregate and not just of the last finger (say, the thumb) to which we happened to point. This is a very abstract idea, and in a way, contradicts the act of counting itself. To get "five," we first pointed to the smallest finger, saying "one"; to the next finger, saying, "two"; and so on until we got to "five." Having done all that counting of individual fingers, we now ignore it. We forget the fact that the smallest finger was called "one" and the thumb "five"; now we shift from individual fingers to the hand as a whole and call the collection of fingers "five."

2. The order of counting does not matter. We started with the smallest finger, carefully counted from left to right until we got to the thumb. Yet we know that had we started with the thumb (or any

other finger), the result would be exactly the same. Again, this is a very abstract idea. Many times order does matter. If you go from Ithaca to New York City the result is clearly different from a journey beginning in New York and ending in Ithaca. We know that the order of counting makes no difference but that the order of traveling does. Why counting has a special status is by no means a trivial question.

3. The things counted need not look alike. The fingers are of course similar one to the other; but we know we could count a collection consisting of one elephant, one finger, one orange, one envelope, one puddle of water, and still get "five."

4. The physical arrangement or appearance of a collection is irrelevant to its number. Five candies in a line are "five" and five candies in a circle are also "five." Making the line into a circle changes the appearance, but not the underlying reality of number. But what is this underlying reality that you cannot see? Again, an abstract idea.

5. In respect to number, a collection of five fingers is the same as five elephants. This is perhaps the most abstract idea of all. Fingers are obviously different from elephants, and yet we insist that in some deeper sense these fingers and elephants are the same. Again, it is an underlying reality, not a surface characteristic, to which we refer.

6. Finally, we know that counting the fingers tells us how many fingers there are. This seems obvious, but what does it mean to know "how many fingers there are?" If we know there are "five," then we also know that we have one more than "four" and one less than "six." We know that if we combined two hands of five fingers each we would have "ten" altogether. In short, we do not just know "five" in isolation: we incorporate "five" into a whole system of knowledge, into our arithmetic.

We see that the meaning of "five" is complex indeed. It is no wonder then that the child's concept of number is different from ours and takes many years to develop.

Children's "five"

The young child's concept of number differs from ours in its extreme emphasis on appearances. Sometimes children apply number words to particular physical arrangements of objects but not to others. At five years of age, Churchill's Steven had painted a picture of a lake with some ducks swimming one behind the other.[15] The teacher looked at the picture and said, "I see you have got five ducks on your pond." Steven looked at the picture in a puzzled way and then said, "It isn't five; there isn't one in the middle." For Steven, "five" referred *only* to an X-shaped array (the arrangement shown in Figure 1–6B). Unlike us, he did not realize that "five" refers to *any* arrangement, including the straight line he drew (Figure 1–6A).*

A: Steven's Ducks

B: Steven's Five

Figure 1–6. *Ducks and ducks*

Similarly, Reiss's Charles was counting his marbles, of which there were four red and one blue.[16] By chance he counted the red marbles first—"one, two, three, four"—and the blue last, so that it was called "five." From that time onward, Charles always called *any* blue marble "five"; that was its name and the name had nothing to do with a number property. Unlike us, Charles did not realize that the last number counted refers to the collection as a whole, not just to the last thing counted.

*There is some evidence that seems to contradict this finding (Gelman, R. How young children reason about small numbers. Paper delivered at the University of Indiana, 1975). Children's notion of equivalence when *very small* numbers of objects are involved—that is, 2 or 3—may not suffer from this overreliance on appearance. If children are shown two objects side by side and are later shown two objects one on top of the other, they recognize the numerical equivalence. What I say in this chapter may hold true only for numbers above 3.

Indeed, number is often treated as a *name*, not a *concept*. Renwick's Moira, a four-year-old, was having tea with her governess, who asked her to count some pieces of bread and butter.[17] Moira correctly counted, "One, two, three." The governess said, "Eat one," and Moira did so. The governess asked, "How many now?" Moira said, "Three." Governess: "But you've eaten one." Moira: "Yes, but two and three are left." For Moira, the counting numbers are names

The Meaning of Number Words in Other Cultures

Number words may contain hidden meanings which give insight into a culture's view of number. Wertheimer[18] suggests that number concepts often reflect certain kinds of naturally occurring events or objects. The notion of "two" may arise in the context of natural pairs like eyes, shoes, or arms. By this logic, a pair of legs may be considered two; but one man and one horse are one rider. This *concept* of two may ultimately lead to a *word* like *twin,* to which the English *two* is related.

In several languages, number reveals an intimate connection with finger counting. In the Sotha language, the word for 5 means "complete the hand" and the word for 6 means "jump"—that is, jump to the other hand.

The Malinke language of Africa uses number words referring to other parts of the body. The word for 9 means "to the one of the belly"—that is, the nine months of pregnancy. The word for 40 is "a mattress." This is an obscure reference to the forty digits of the husband and wife who lie on the same mattress.[19]

The Themshian language of British Columbia is extremely concrete. "There we find seven distinct sets of number words: one for flat objects and animals; one for counting people; one for long objects and one for canoes; one for measures; one for counting when no definite object is referred to."[20]

Sometimes the investigation of number words is fraught with peril. The French explorer, Labillardière, investigated counting among the Tonga Islanders and found that they could easily reach 100,000. Not satisfied with this, the Frenchman asked them to go on and got what he thought were numerals into the billions. Yet later examination showed that these "numerals" were "partly nonsense words and partly indelicate expressions, so that the supposed series of high numerals forms at once a little vocabulary of Tongan indecency, and a warning as to the probable results of taking down unchecked answers from question-worried savages."[21] The savages seem to have outsmarted the anthropologist here.

for individual objects; for us, they are a means to an end, namely discovering the number property of the set as a whole.

Churchill's Catherine used number names in a somewhat different way.[22] One day she went for a walk with friends. After a time, she said, "I'll count us." She pointed to a friend and said, "one"; to another friend and said, "two." Finally, she pointed to herself and said, "three." She was puzzled. "That's wrong, I'm four. I'll try again. One, two, three. But I'm still four. You try."

Catherine believed in number as a very special and unique name. People can have one number name and one only. Her number name was "four" because she was four years old, and it was impossible that she could be called anything else.

Young children also believe that the order in which objects are counted makes a difference concerning the final number value. If you count a line of objects from left to right, you get "five"; but if you count from right to left you may get some other number entirely. At 4–6, Charles was counting pills arranged in a line.[23] He started at one end, counted to "five," and then counted once more from the other end, again getting "five." After the second counting, he exclaimed in amazement, "Now *this* is one, two, three, four, five!" It is not at all obvious to young children that the order of counting is irrelevant to number.

Nor is it obvious that counting tells how many things there are in a set. Suppose the child is asked to count a set and does so correctly, getting "seven" as the result. Is "seven" just a word or does it communicate to the child how many there are? Suppose the collection of objects is now covered and the child is asked, "How many are there?" At three years of age, most children try to count the set again or make up a number; but they cannot say "seven" even though they have just counted the set.[24]

We see then that a child may count things correctly but fail to make use of this information in the same way that we do. *Number words do not necessarily convey correct number ideas.* A most striking example of this involves Deborah. At six years of age (a year after the observation on counting fingers), she was given Piaget's conservation of number problem.

The interviewer placed seven playing cards in a line.

I: How many cards?

D: Seven.

I: Make another line of cards that's the same number.

Deborah counted out seven cards—"one, two, three, four, five, six, seven"—and placed them in line directly above the interviewer's (Figure 1–7).

The interviewer pointed to the bottom row, saying it was his, and to the top row, identifying it as Deborah's.

Deborah's row

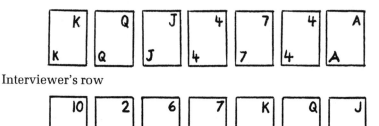

Interviewer's row

Figure 1–7. *Two lines of cards*

I: Now does your line have just as many as my line? Is it just as many cards?

D: Yes.

I: All right, now watch what I do with my line.

The interviewer spread out his row of cards as Deborah watched. This is the "conservation" problem. The question is whether the child *conserves* the initial equivalence despite the change in mere appearance (Figure 1–8).

Deborah's row

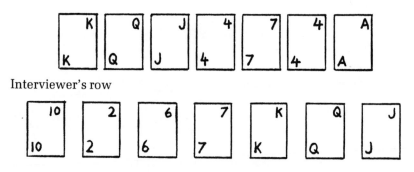

Interviewer's row

Figure 1–8. *The cards transformed*

I: See. Now do we both have as many cards? Does this line have as many cards as this line?

Deborah shook her head to indicate no.

I: No? Which line has more?

Deborah pointed to the interviewer's line.

I: Why does that line have more?

D: Because it is out to here [meaning, the interviewer's line was longer than hers].

I: O.K. I see . . . but how many cards are in my line?

D: Seven.

I: How many cards are in your line?

D: Seven.

I: How come this one has more if they both have seven?

D: Because you spread them out.

So the length of the rows is more influential in determining the child's judgment of number than is counting. If this has "seven" and that has "seven," they are not necessarily the same number!

The interviewer then proceeded to make Deborah's line longer.

I: Now let's move it like this. Does your line have as many cards as my line?

D: No.

I: How come?

D: 'Cause mine is stretched out.

I: Does your line have more or does my line have more?

D: [Deborah pointed to herself.] 'Cause I spread mine out.

Then the interviewer established that there were seven elements in each line, but again she insisted that her line had more because it was spread out.

The interviewer then introduced a variation on the conservation procedure. First he made the two lines equal in number and also in length. Deborah agreed that both had the same number. Then:

I: Watch this. I take another card and I put it in my line and I spread yours out.

This resulted in eight cards in the interviewer's shorter line and seven in Deborah's longer line.

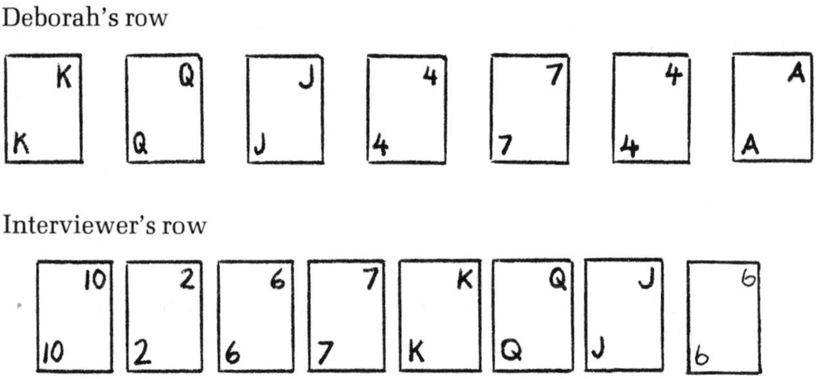

Deborah's row

Interviewer's row

Figure 1–9. *A sneaky variation*

I: Now do we both have the same?

D: No.

I: Who has more?

Deborah indicated herself.

I: Who has more? You have more?

D: 'Cause I spread mine out.

Next the investigator asked Deborah to count the elements of both sets several times. At this point Deborah began to waiver, apparently in conflict. Sometimes she maintained that the interviewer had more and sometimes that she did.

At about age six or seven in Western cultures (and at different ages in other cultures), children learn to conserve. They come to believe that rearrangement of sets affects only their appearance, not their number. When this change in thought takes place, then children can appreciate the meaning of the counting numbers; then they can realize that seven here is the same as seven there. *Maturity of thought helps children to understand number words; words do not guarantee logical thought.*

SUMMARY

The adult's concept of cardinal number is more complex than is usually recognized. To the adult, a word like "five" describes a property of a collection as a whole. Adults recognize that the order in which they count a collection of objects does not matter, and that things need not look alike in order to be counted together. They know too that the physical arrangement or appearance of a collection is irrelevant to its number, and that sets containing quite different objects—elephants and ants—can be identical in number property. Finally, for the adult, a number does not exist in isolation: it is part of a larger system of knowledge concerning arithmetic.

Young children's concept of number can be different from our own. Sometimes they use number words in connection with some physical arrangements but not with others: three objects in a triangle qualify as "three"; the same objects in a line do not. Also, young children treat number as a name rather than as a concept describing a characteristic of a set. Whichever object of a set happens to have been counted last is called "five"; "five" does not refer to the set as a whole. Similarly, children fail to realize that the order of counting objects makes no difference and even that counting tells you how many objects there are altogether in a collection. The limited nature of children's understanding is vividly illustrated by cases in which they count objects with perfect accuracy and yet make completely erroneous number judgments concerning those same objects. Thus, for example, they realize that there are "seven" here and "seven" there but think that one group has a greater number of elements than the other.

PRINCIPLES

1. *The accurate use of words does not guarantee understanding.* Children can say the counting words correctly; they can even enumerate objects accurately; yet at the same time their understanding of those words and of that counting may be quite different from our own. They mouth the words but garble the concept. There are three things here, but "three" always must take the form of a triangle. The apparent meaning of children's words can give a distorted view of their true understanding. In the intellectual realm, as in the emotional, one must listen with "the third ear" to apprehend the underlying meaning of children's language.

2. *Children's thought can be qualitatively different from the adult's.* For the adult it is inconceivable that "three" be limited to the case of triangles or to the third thing counted. But for children all this is commonplace. Their concepts, their very ways of reasoning, can be different from our own. One of Piaget's great contributions is to have demonstrated this difference in many areas, from children's concept of number to their moral judgment. It is no longer safe to assume that children's thought is but a paler version of the adult's.

Chapter 2

Concepts in Babies and Little Children

We have examined counting, an obviously mathematical activity. Now we shall get a glimpse into children's secret mathematical life. Young children develop informal and often unrecognized concepts of mathematics. They have notions of "more," "same," and "adding." Even babies possess elementary mathematical ideas.

BABY MATHEMATICS

In our daily lives, we are continually faced with problems of quantity. As the philosopher Whitehead put it:

> Through and through the world is infected with quantity. To talk sense is to talk in quantities. It is no use saying that the nation is large—How large? It is no use saying that radium is scarce—How scarce? You cannot evade quantity. You may fly to poetry and music, and quantity and number will face you in your rhythms and your octaves.[1]

Quantity does not "infect" the world only through rhythms and octaves; it manifests itself in more homely ways as well. Consider how thoroughly quantity fills the world of infants. They lie in cribs with a certain number of bars. The walls in their rooms display repetitions of bricks or wooden boards or regularity in the pattern of the wallpaper. Their parents go into the room and out of it over and over again. Some of their toys are bigger than others; some are identical and others are equivalent in size. If they push a toy, it moves; and the harder they push, the harder it moves. Infants thus have ample opportunity to learn about number, repetition, regularity, differences in magnitude, equivalence, causality, and correlation.

While quantity surrounds infants, do they notice any of it and, if so, to which aspects are they sensitive? A number of observations suggest that infants *perceive* certain quantitative features of the world. Preyer, a German psychologist, reports the following observation concerning his son at ten months of age.[2] The baby had a set of nine bowling pins, each identical to the other. One day, without the baby's seeing it, one of the bowling pins was removed, so that only eight remained. The baby glanced at the toys and indicated by his displeasure that he knew something was amiss. The baby saw that something was *different;* this set of bowling pins was not the same as the one he was familiar with.

Quantity in the Environment

It is obvious that there are differences in the extent to which quantity "infects" different environments. Some cultures stress formal education while others lack it. Some cultures stress educational toys while in others they are absent. In some cultures effective use of quantitative skills is virtually necessary to survival. Thus, even unschooled members of the Dioula, a mercantile tribe in Ivory Coast, are relatively adept at aspects of practical arithmetic useful in the market place. By contrast, members of farming groups living nearby fail to achieve a comparable level of sophistication, perhaps because their culture does not demand it.

While some cultures suffer from the quantity infection more than others, all environments exhibit certain basic aspects of quantity. What culture lacks things to count, or objects that are bigger than others, or things that cause other things to act? What culture, in short, does not exist in the natural world? In view of this, it is hard to see how *any* child, rich or poor, Western or non-Western, can grow up in an environment which does not offer him or her the *natural opportunity* to learn about basic aspects of quantity. In this sense, environments are all similar and quantity is universally available. We shall see later that there is a sense in which all children take advantage of this natural opportunity.

Infants' concern with quantity is reflected in their earliest words.[3] One of the first words for many babies is *more* or *'nother.* At twenty-one months, after playing with a doll, Bloom's Katherine saw a collection of similar dolls and said, "more doll." Her language seemed to make a distinction between the *one* doll she had been playing with and the larger collection. At twenty-five months, Bloom's Eric picked up one clown and then another. "Two clowns," he exclaimed. Babies find the world of quantity so important that they must describe it in words.[4]

Even more surprising, babies seem to see how quantitative events relate to one another. At three months, Piaget's Laurent was playing with a chain attached to rattles. By accident, he pulled the chain and it caused the rattles to sound. He grasped the chain and began to swing it very gently; this made the rattles produce a very soft sound. "Laurent then definitely increases by degrees his own movements: he shakes the chain more and more vigorously." This of course produces increasingly loud sounds in the rattles. "[He] laughs uproariously at the result obtained. On seeing the child's expression it is impossible not to deem this gradation intentional."[5] The infant seemed to know that the harder he shook the chain, the louder the sound would be. The infant can see complex relations in his environment.

Another example involves size and weight.[6] Suppose the infant (around one year of age) is shown a series of brass rods, increasing in both length and weight. Thus, one rod may be three inches long and ten ounces; the second, five inches long, fifteen ounces; the third, seven inches long, twenty ounces; and so on. Just as Laurent could learn that as force increases so does sound, here the baby could discover that as length increases so does weight; both cases involve a relation between quantitative properties. Given the opportunity to play with these rods, the infant learns to use length to anticipate weight. He sees how long a rod is, and from that predicts how heavy it will be. This anticipation is shown by the fact that he picks up each rod with just the right amount of effort. If the rod is long (and therefore, he predicts, heavy), he uses a lot of force to lift it; if it is short, he applies a minimum of effort.

Other observations suggest that the baby can inject quantity into his behavior. Piaget reports that at nine months his son Laurent "imitates the sounds which he knows how to make spontaneously. I say *papa* to him, he replies *papa* or *baba*. When I say *papa-papa* he replies *apapa* or *ababa*. When I say *papa papa papapa* [seven *pas*] he replies *papapapa* [four *pas*]."[7] While his imitation is not perfect, Laurent nevertheless could reliably make different numbers of sounds.

An experiment with four-month-old babies makes a similar point.[8] Babies learned to make a certain number of responses in order to get a reward, specifically the opportunity to see some flashing, colored lights. For example, on one occasion, the babies learned to turn their head two times to the left in order to see the lights; on another occasion, they learned to alternate turns to the left and right. Of course, when the task demands became too complex, the babies failed: they could not learn to turn their head twice to the left followed by three times to the right.

We see then that babies can reliably perform certain numbers of responses—either as an act of imitation or to get something they want. The infants' action contains quantity, just as their perception is sensitive to it. These capabilities seem to prepare them for living in a world of quantity.

THE YOUNG CHILD

Quantitative concepts continue to develop from age two to six. During this time, the child has notions of "more" and "less," "same," and "adding." Children's concepts and skills are largely implicit, informal, and nonverbal: they cannot talk mathematics explicitly. Consider first Alfred Binet's work on the notions of "more" and "less."

More and less

From age two to six, young children's thoughts are in many ways something of an enigma. On the one hand, some of their mathematical concepts are remarkably insightful; they allow children to deal effectively with quantitative problems and even provide the foundation for later mathematical ideas. On the other hand, many of their concepts involve unusual—even bizarre—patterns of thought that often lead children into error on problems that to the adult seem trivially simple. One example of this quality of thought involves the notions of "more" and "less."

Alfred Binet, famous (or infamous) as the inventor of the first successful intelligence test, made some fascinating observations concerning his young daughter's judgments of more and less.[9] Binet presented Madeleine, at 4–4, with a series of problems, each involving the comparison of two collections. The collections contained similar objects—coins, tokens, bean seeds, and so on—laid flat and close to one another on the table, as in Figure 2–1. The objects were in a haphazard, unplanned arrangement. Madeleine's task was to point to the group having more than the other.

At this stage in her development, Madeleine could only *count*

Set 1   Set 2

Figure 2–1. *Two sets of coins*

up to three objects. Nevertheless, she did amazingly well on Binet's task. Comparisons of 5 versus 7 presented no difficulty. Madeleine could sometimes even identify the greater when 18 versus 17 was involved!

Observations of large numbers of children give similar results.[10] Young children were shown a series of two paper plates, on each of which were arranged a collection of marbles. Each collection varied in number from 1 to 13. Thus, a child might see 3 versus 5 marbles or 7 versus 13. The child's task was to decide, *within two seconds*, which plate had "more." Younger children (three to four years of age) got about two thirds of the problems correct, whereas the older children (four to five years of age) got about five sixths correct. These results support Binet's conclusion that young children can make fairly accurate judgments concerning which set has more.

In Ivory Coast, West Africa, schooled and unschooled children do equally well on tasks requiring judgments of "more" and "less." Moreover, the African children perform at about the same level as American children of the same age. All do well on Binet's problems.

The informal judgment of more and less may well be universal. But how do children do it? One possibility is counting. If counting is done carefully, it always leads to a perfect solution of the task. But Binet's daughter could count only to 3, and the other young children were prevented from counting by the requirement to give a decision within two seconds.

How, then, were the problems solved? According to Binet, Madeleine's judgment was based on the relative space covered by the two collections. She designated as "more" the set that covered the larger area. To test this idea. Binet showed Madeleine a set of small tokens and a set of large ones (as in Figure 2–2). The set of small tokens had a greater number of elements but covered less area than did the set of large ones. If Madeleine used area to reach her decision then she should maintain that the set of large tokens was "more."

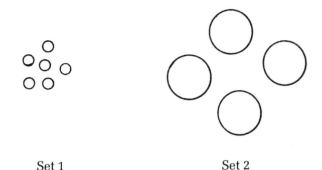

Set 1   Set 2

More numerous, lesser   Less numerous, greater
area   area

Figure 2–2.   *Small and large tokens*

Binet's results showed that this was so: under most conditions Madeleine consistently designated as "more" the set that took up *more space,* even when it had *fewer elements.* (Posner's research shows that the same is true in Ivory Coast.)

The judgment of "more" nicely illustrates the complexity of early thought. Children are faced with a difficult situation: they must determine which of two unequal collections has more even though they cannot count to solve the problem. Given this limitation, their procedure is entirely sensible. They decide that the set covering the greater area is the more numerous. This method for judging more *usually* leads to success, since it is *usually* (but not always) true that the greater the area, the greater the number. So children's intuition is generally sound.

At the same time, their distinctive way of thinking about more and less can lead to error under certain circumstances. Young children believe that the collection that *appears* to have more *really does.* They must trust appearances since they have no way (like counting) of dealing with the reality. But appearances often deceive, and their intuition therefore is only partially adequate. Like Madeleine, children make incorrect judgments when the smaller area is the more numerous. They make errors too when large numbers of objects are involved. Perhaps children can perceive the difference in area between a set of 17 and a set of 18, but it would be almost impossible to see the difference between 118 versus 117. Success with large numbers demands more precise methods, like counting, that these young children cannot employ.

Same: Piaget's conservation problem

In chapter 1, we saw that counting does not help children to understand the idea of sameness or conservation. Now we shall explore the reasons for this failure: As with their notion of "more," young children's intuition of sameness relies on appearances, not reality. Sometimes this is an effective procedure, sometimes not.

Piaget has done many fascinating investigations into the stages of children's notion of "same."[11] His work has led to major insights and has resulted in educational programs.

In one study, Piaget showed the child, Don, 4–1, a row of five beans, and asked him to create another collection of beans with the same number as the model. First, Don grabbed a handful of beans at random, and by chance took 5. He arranged them in a row that was longer than the model. Seeing the difference in length, Don said that his row had more. The interviewer urged him to make the rows the same number. Don responded by putting out seven objects in a line that was the same length as the model. He maintained, "They're exactly the same."

According to Piaget, Don is in Stage I. He believed that if two lines of beans are the same length, they have the same number. If the lines are of different lengths, they are unequal in number. He based his judgments on the physical appearance of things and ignored real number. This is analogous to Binet's finding that judgments of "more" are based on physical variables like area.

At the next stage of development, Stage II, the young child, at about five years of age, seems to have mastered this problem. Asked to construct a set having the same number as a model, the child is at first quite accurate.

Consider the example of Jonathan at 4–6.

I: Jonathan, you watch what I'm going to do. I'm going to put out these little dolls (Figure 2–3). Now what I'd like you to do is to put out just as many hats as there are dolls—the same number of hats as dolls.

Figure 2–3. *Dolls wanting hats*

Jonathan placed one hat below each doll.

I: Are there the same number now?

J: Yes.

At this point it appears that Jonathan understood "same": he used the method of one-to-one correspondence to construct equal sets. But consider what happened next. The interviewer gave Jonathan Piaget's famous conservation problem. As Jonathan watched, the interviewer made the line of dolls longer than the line of hats. That is, he rearranged one of the sets so that it *looked* different from the other, but its number was unchanged (Figure 2–4). The question was whether the child would recognize that the equivalance between the two sets is *conserved* despite the irrelevant change in appearance.

Figure 2–4. *Dolls separated from hats*

I: Are there more dolls now or more hats or just the same number?

J: More dolls.

The interviewer then returned each doll to its position above each hat, and Jonathan agreed that the numbers were again the same. Next, the interviewer spread the *hats* apart. Now Jonathan indicated that there were more hats!

While the child in this stage correctly uses one-to-one correspondence to construct equal sets, his procedure leads to a fragile judgment. When the rows no longer *look* the same, be believes one has more—he fails to conserve.

Could his error have been the result of a mere misunderstanding of the instructions? The interviewer next showed Jonathan two rows of candies, one designated as his and the other as the interviewer's. The rows were identical in appearance (phase 1, in Figure 2–5).

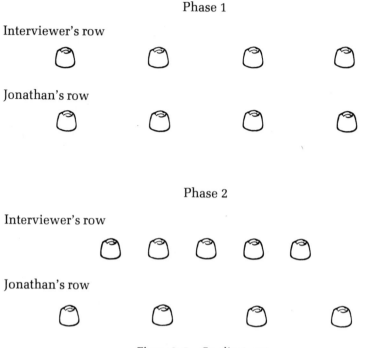

Figure 2–5. *Candies to eat*

After Jonathan agreed that the rows were the same, the interviewer said; "Now watch what I do: I move yours out and I put one here." The interviewer added one to his own row and spread Jonathan's apart (phase 2 in Figure 2–5). Next the interviewer asked, "Which one do you want to eat?" The question was posed in this way to increase the child's motivation and at the same time avoid the use of words like "more" and "same." Surely he can comprehend instructions about eating. If the child really understands number, then this technique should demonstrate his knowledge, whereas a verbal procedure might fail.

In response to the question, Jonathan indicated that he would like to eat his row, the longer but less numerous set.

I: That one? Why do you want to eat that one?

J: 'Cause you put these out [meaning, because you spread these out].

Clearly Jonathan was responding to length just as Madeleine based her judgment on area.

Suppose the child now counts the objects. Does that help?

I: Can you count them for me?

J: 1, 2, 3, 4.

I: So you have 4. And how many do I have?

J: 1, 2, 3, 4, 5.

I: So who has more?

J: Me.

I: You? But this one has 4 and this one has 5.

J: You put yours like that [meaning the interviewer's line was shorter] and put mine right there [that is, spread it out].

So counting does not help Jonathan, just as it did not help Deborah to deal with a similar problem. The child's judgment is based on appearances. If they look the same, then they *are* the same. If they look different, then they *are* different. Again, this method leads to some successes and some failures.

In Stage III, at around age six or seven, children solve the Piagetian conservation problem. Shown the two rows of elements, they say that they are the same despite the difference in appearance because "You didn't add any or take any away," or "You just spread them apart," or "You could put them back together again and they could look the same." Moreover, they are so confident in their judgment as to be surprised at the very question. They say, "Are you kidding? *Of course*, they're the same."

Virtually all children learn to conserve. In Western societies everyone, except for the severely retarded, eventually succeeds at the task. Some children may master it as early as four or five, others at six, and still others not until eight or nine. But all eventually achieve success.

Moreover, the presence or absence of this ability does not seem to depend on schooling. For one thing, some children develop conservation before they have been to school at all, or very early in their school careers. For another, research shows that Black American children who were not allowed to attend school (because of a dispute over desegregation) nevertheless managed to develop successful conservation.[12] Formal education may not be required to teach children the basic thought processes that Piaget has described.

Addition and subtraction without counting

It is not until age six that children succeed at conservation. Addition and subtraction seem to be easier. Young children experience many instances of adding and subtracting in the natural

Cross-cultural Studies of Piagetian Notions

Children all over the world display the developmental trends that Piaget uncovered in Swiss children. In rural Thailand, for example, children exhibit the typical stages of conservation and justify their answers in virtually the same words used by Swiss children.[13] Does this mean that Piagetian stages are innate and simply unfold with biological maturation? No. Cultural experiences affect the ages at which children attain conservation. Something about the experience of living in rural Thailand, for instance, slows down the process of learning conservation. On the other hand, children in the Mexican State of Jalisco, which is famous for its pottery making, are advanced in their ability to conserve substance.[14] (Conservation of substance is a task in which the child is asked to determine first whether two clay balls that look alike contain the same amount of clay, and second, whether the amount remains the same after one ball has been flattened to look like a pancake.) In Jalisco, the cultural experience of working with clay seems to accelerate the development of conservation of substance. So the Piagetian stages are extremely widespread, but this does not mean they are influenced only by biological factors.

setting. They have some food on their plates and their parents give them more; they have some toys and their brother or sister takes one away. These experiences afford the opportunity for developing intuitions about addition and subtraction.

Common observation shows that children prefer addition to subtraction: they generally like to get things, not to lose them. This preference indicates that they see a distinction between addition and subtraction, but it is not clear how much they understand of each.

Fortunately, there is some interesting research on the issue.[15] Suppose the young child is shown two collections of eight coins each. Each collection is in a row and both rows look the same. The child judges that the collections have the same number, probably because their appearances are identical. The interviewer places each collection in a separate box so that the child can no longer see the coins. Next the interviewer takes a new coin, as the child watches, and places it in a box, the one on the child's right, for example. Which box has more coins, or do they both still have the same number? Notice what the problem is from the child's point of view. The child knows at the outset that both boxes contain the same number of coins, although they cannot be seen. The only visible event is the placing of a new coin in a box. The question therefore is whether the child realizes that the addition of an object to one of two equal sets makes that set have more than the other. Research shows that almost all children at ages four and five have no difficulty with this kind of problem or an analogous subtraction problem (taking one coin from a box).

Suppose that the child is given a somewhat more complex problem. After an equal number of objects has been placed in each box, the interviewer places *two* objects in the left box and *one* in the right. Which box has more? Again, almost all children at ages four and five solves this problem (and an analogous subtraction problem).

Next, the interviewer makes the problem still more difficult. The child first sees different numbers of coins in each collection. One set of coins has 16 and the other has 12. The child correctly identifies which has more. The larger collection is then placed in the left box and the smaller in the right. The interviewer adds one coin to the box on the right. Which has more, the left box (16) or the right (12 + 1)?

We used this problem to see if young children are confused about the concept of addition. They might believe that when you add to a set it always has more than another; they might forget to compare the two sets. In a way, this is what may happen during feeding. Children finish their ice cream and ask for more. When they get it, they have more than they just had (which was nothing since they had eaten all of it), but they do not necessarily have more than their older sister. Perhaps as a result of this experience, they identify adding with "more than I had before." This is of course a very limited notion of addition and its consequences.

The problem just described (16 versus 12 + 1) can identify children who use the strategy of "when you add to a set, it always has more than another." Children doing this should think that 12 + 1 has more than 16. Most children (19 of 26 tested) at four and five years of age do not use this immature strategy; they are not fooled by our unusual problem. The average child at this age has sound intuitions about elementary addition and subtraction.

SUMMARY

Even infants possess intuitions concerning number. Quantity pervades their world and they are sensitive to it. They perceive differences in number and use some of their first words to comment on them. They notice and even anticipate complex relationships among variables in their environment. Moreover, they can inject quantity. into their behavior by controlling the number of responses they make.

During the years two to six, young children develop relatively effective ways of dealing with problems of more and less. Without counting, they can make fairly accurate judgments concerning which of two sets has more, at least when relatively small numbers of elements are involved. They manage to do this by basing their judgment on physical appearances. In general, this strategy works, since the physical variables they use are, in fact, correlated with number. But young children's strategy often fails, since the correlation is imperfect. They require a more precise method, like counting, but are not yet capable of it.

Young children's notion of sameness also relies on appearances, not reality. Piaget's studies show that at Stage I children believe that any two sets are the same in number if they look the same. Asked to construct a collection that will be the same number as a model, children make a collection of the same length (or shape) as the model, but not necessarily the same number. In Stage II, children can use the method of one-to-one correspondence to construct a set having the same appearance and number as a model. But when one of the sets is manipulated so as to change only its appearance, children fail to recognize that the number is the same—that the equivalence has been conserved across the visible changes. Neither counting nor clearer instructions seem to help the Stage II child solve this task. In Stage III, children solve the problem and in fact believe that the answer is obvious and should not pose a problem to anyone. Children do not seem to need schooling to develop the ability to conserve.

Young children experience many instances of adding and taking away in their natural environment. They see a difference between the two, and at an early age achieve an elementary appreciation of the operations of addition and subtraction. They know, for example, that adding to a set makes it have more than it had before but not necessarily more than another set. Thus, 3 + 1 is not greater than 5.

PRINCIPLES

1. *Before entrance to school, children possess important concepts and skills concerning mathematics.* Even babies may see that there is more here than there, or that this variable relates to that.

These judgments are crude but they seem to be genuinely quantitative. From years two to six, young children's informal skills yield a surprising degree of accuracy with respect to judgments of "more" and "less," "same," and "addition," at least under certain conditions. Obviously, the baby and young child do not know mathematics in any formal, symbolic, or verbal sense. Their mathematical knowledge is like their knowledge of distance. They can judge accurately that this is closer than that but cannot say how they did it; in fact, they are most often unaware of having made the judgment. So the child's early mathematics is informal, implicit, unconscious, and nonverbal. It is *intuitive*.

2. *Young children's mathematical intuition demonstrates strengths at the same time as it suffers from weaknesses.* Young children base a judgment of "more" on a physical variable like length or area. Since such variables are correlated with number, children's judgments are often correct. But since the correlation is imperfect, they are sometimes wrong. Children's *techniques* are consistent—they always base their judgment on a physical variable—but this leads to inconsistent *results*—sometimes they are right, sometimes wrong. Piaget has himself recognized this inconsistency; unfortunately, his followers sometimes focus mainly on young children's weaknesses rather than on their strengths.

Chapter 3

Learning Practical Arithmetic

We have seen how young children learn to count and how they acquire concepts of number. Now we will see how they learn to combine the counting and concepts into a practical arithmetic.

LEARNING: WHY AND HOW

Children learn to *see* that the numbers from 1 to 9 follow 30 and 40 and 50 in just the same order as they follow 20. They learn to do finger counting with facility so that they can determine the number of relatively large sets. They learn to *understand* what number means—for example, that "five" in this arrangement is the same as "five" in that. Children's learning involves more than memorizing facts: indeed much of their memorizing is in the service of seeing, doing, and understanding.

Now we must ask, *why* do they engage in these kinds of learning? What motivates children to learn informal arithmetic? Early learning seems easier and pleasanter than the school learning that takes place in later years. Why is this so?

Next we must inquire into *how* children go about learning. For the most part, adults do not teach young children informal mathematics. Children seem to learn it on their own. But how do they accomplish this? In what sense is their learning self-directed? And what role does the parent (or other agents of culture like television or books) play in the process?

Why children learn

One motive for learning informal arithmetic is *practical utility*. Children learn to count or to add because it is useful for them to do so. In their everyday activities outside of school, children tend to use arithmetic (defined broadly) as they carry out transactions in stores, read page numbers in books, divide food with playmates and pets, and play board games like *Monopoly*.[1] Deborah, Rebecca, and Jonathan frequently used measuring cups to distribute equally among themselves various liquid substances (like soda); they eagerly learned to tell time and to read times in the television listings; they tried to add up mentally the prices of items in the store and to determine whether the total was more or less than their savings, and if so, how much, so that they could either buy more or ask for more, as the case might be. Greg, an eight-year-old, is adept at the mental addition of his parents' and their friends' *Perquacky* (a word game) scores, which can reach 5,000. In all these cases, arithmetic solves a very real, everyday problem that concerns the child. This kind of arithmetic is *useful*.

Practical Necessity in the Ancient World and in Tribal Africa

Practical necessity had a strong influence on the early development of mathematics. For example, written number may have developed as early as 3000 B.C. in Mesopotamia, where the Sumerians invented written symbols to keep their accounts.[2] At about the same time, the Egyptians had a flourishing economy that required keeping commercial and government records involving large numbers. Therefore, they developed a series of hieroglyphics to express large numbers up to hundreds of thousands.

Among the Kpelle of Liberia, a good deal of mathematics centers around rice, which is the basis for the local economy. Rice is measured in many different and elaborate ways. "They have no other system with such internal coherence and complexity. This makes eminently good sense since rice is the staple of the diet. The centrality of rice to the diet, and to the culture itself, is underlined in this measurement system. . . ."[3] The Kpelle can more accurately estimate the number of units of rice in a large jar than can Americans. Furthermore, various specialists in Kpelle society are adept at the mathematical operations required for their trade, whereas the ordinary person may not be. A trader uses a good deal of mental addition; a farmer may not.

James Herdon provides a dramatic instance of such motivation. His junior high school students found it extremely difficult to learn arithmetic (and almost anything else) in school. Despite Herdon's best efforts to motivate them, to make mathematics interesting, they could not, or would not, learn. They were known as the "dumb class," and there seemed to be every reason for believing this description to be accurate. One day, however, Herdon happened to visit the bowling alley where the dumb class gathered after school. He discovered that the dumbest kid had a job there keeping score for the bowlers.

"He was keeping score. Two teams, four people on each, eight bowling scores at once. Adding quickly, not making mistakes (for no one was going to put up with errors), following the rather complicated process of scoring in the game of bowling . . . the bowling league is not a welfare organization nor part of Headstart and wasn't interested in giving some dumb kid a chance to improve himself. . . . No, they were giving this smart kid who had proved to be fast and accurate fifteen dollars because they could use a good scorer."[4]

Another kind of motivation is what psychologists call intrinsic. This refers to activities that are done for their own sakes or for the fun of it, in the absence of any clear external reward or practical necessity. Here the activity itself is fun (and so the motivation is said to be intrinsic to the activity) and the child is not concerned with whether it leads to some external goal or reward.

Court reports that ever since her son Paul began to talk, he showed immense interest in numbers.

He always delighted in counting, and whenever there was any danger of his becoming impatient with the process of combing his curls or dressing him, he would be kept quiet by either a story or a verse, or counting. As soon as his interest in numbers became apparent, much attention was given to his efforts in this direction, and help, when asked for directly or when the need for it was evident, came forth abundantly and willingly. Often his attention was called to the numbers of blocks picked out for construction, to the number of plates at dinner, etc. But he was never forced to count, and every new step in his arithmetic development was undertaken by him without any outside stimulus. Thus although encouragement was never lacking, whatever he learned in regard to numbers, space, and time was practically self-taught.[5]

Thus, while the parents helped the child when he asked for it or seemed to need it, the basic interest in counting seemed to stem from the child himself. At twenty months, Paul used to point to objects, name them, and then immediately look around for corresponding objects to count. For example, the child would name and point to a lamp, look for another lamp, and then say "two" lamps. It is hard to see how this kind of activity can be motivated by practical necessity.

At four years, Paul was especially interested in counting and did it over and over again, naming the numbers one after another until he was out of breath. Several times he actually counted to 1,000, one by one. It is again implausible to suppose that practical necessity could be involved in such activity.

Paul's spontaneous interest was not limited to counting. He became fascinated with addition, and would engage in various self-invented addition games with his mother. For example, he would bring his mother three blocks, ask whether she wanted four, and then bring one more to achieve the desired result.

Similarly, Donald, at 4–6, one day began to add the spots on some cards. "I want to see what 5 and 2 make," he said. He counted all the spots on both cards, sometimes starting with the larger number, sometimes with the smaller. He soon even tried to add up the dots on three cards. On another occasion, he was playing with twelve blocks. "Look, there are two sixes in twelve . . . and there are six twos." Asked to see what else he could find, he discovered "that three fours and four threes make twelve. In all, he had spent at least an hour and a half at work."[6]

In general, Court's Paul chose by himself the problems in arithmetic that he wanted to solve and learn about. "In all his career as a youthful student of arithmetic the choice of the particular subject was his, mostly to my surprise and even disapproval. He chose himself the particular step in his study of arithmetic at the given time."*[7]

While Paul's interest in arithmetic may have been intrinsic, he often went on to use the knowledge gained in various practical situations. "He always uses most of his arithmetical knowledge in work and play, applying it as soon as he gets it." Court goes on to say that this is perhaps "the explanation of the surprising fact that he hardly forgets what he has learned in arithmetic."[8] Both forms of motivation, intrinsic and practical necessity, exist side by side. Sometimes children learn for one reason, and sometimes for the other. And they apply what they learn in one situation to the other.

Children's intrinsic interest in mathematics can be much more powerful than is ordinarily supposed. At their eleventh birthday

---

*Court's experience with her child is like mine with Deborah, Rebecca, and Jonathan. They became interested in various problems on their own. When this happened they were often encouraged and given help. This may have accelerated their development to some degree. But, in general, their quantitative thinking and arithmetic seem quite typical: the same phenomena and trends have been observed in other children by writers like Court, Pollio and Whittacre, Renwick, and others. The reader can easily verify these phenomena in his or her own children or students.

party, Deborah and Rebecca received a number of gifts, including electronic calculators. After opening the presents, the children and two friends chose to play with the calculators, rather than new toys or games, for almost the entire remainder of the party. They invented a game in which one child would attempt to add several numbers mentally while another child would check the sum on the calculator.

Children's spontaneous interests can take unexpected forms. At nine years of age, Deborah was in a class that emphasized the learning of arithmetic through various games that the children could play on their own. In addition, children were given the supplementary task of completing worksheets containing simple written arithmetic problems like $17 + 8 = ?$ For most children, the games are probably more enjoyable than the worksheets. But this was not true for Deborah. She loved to do the worksheets, much to the dismay of her father who was until then a firm believer in the power of games as a motivator of interest in arithmetic. For Deborah, the repetitive solution of written problems on a worksheet was—for some reason—intrinsically satisfying. It is often hard to predict what will capture the child's spontaneous interest. No doubt, the content of intrinsic motivation differs considerably among children: some like games, some written work, some calculators.

How children learn

Suppose children want to learn some arithmetic. How do they go about it? What role does culture (parents, television, books) play in the process?

Children's learning in the natural environment is largely a self-directed process. At 6–0, Rebecca was sitting on the living room floor playing with her doll and bottle. Earlier, her sister had been playing with cards on the floor, and had spoken some numbers. Now Rebecca started to count, at first by tens. She said, "10, 20, 30, 40, 50, 60, 70, 80, 90, 100, 200, 201, 202, 203, 204. I'm counting a different way, Daddy." A few seconds later she repeated the sequence, counting by tens, then hundreds, and then saying the numbers after 200 one by one. Soon she claimed, "I can count to millions."

This episode exhibits two interesting features that seem typical of learning in the natural setting. One is that Rebecca was engaged in self-motivated practice. She wanted to learn to count and she decided to practice it. It is not true that left to their own devices children are incapable of self-discipline or hard work. *If* they want to learn, they are capable of practice. A second feature is that Rebecca insisted on attempting a difficult problem: she tried to count to the very high numbers that were causing her difficulty. Children do not simply stop at what they are comfortable with; they do not merely repeat what they know. Rather they push on to newer problems. Rebecca even knew quite consciously that she was engaged in something new: "I'm counting in a different way." Children get bored with the familiar and are curious about the novel.

Learning to Print

Several years ago, in collaboration with Mary Wheeler and Edward Tulis, I did a study of the natural development of printing in middle- and lower-class children. The results show that learning to print proceeds in the same kind of self-directed fashion as learning number.

We observed children's printing in a kindergarten class that was relatively unstructured and did not give instruction in printing. In this class, children freely chose activities to work at: blocks; house corner; science (microscopes, balances, etc.); and writing and reading. There were picture dictionaries, paper and pencil, books, and a notebook for each child. The children were free to do as they pleased in the reading and writing area. They could look at pictures, draw, read, or write. If they asked for help they were given it.

What kind of writing did children do under these circumstances? They made letters and words in their notebooks. They put considerable effort into their work, devoting to writing an average of about fifteen minutes each time they worked at their notebooks. They drilled themselves, writing *aaa bbb ccc* or *ball ball ball*. They tried to print only a few letters at a time and then went on to more. The quality of their letters improved over the course of the year. Moreover, there were no significant social class differences in any of these activities. Poor children learned as well as those who were middle-class.[9]

This shows that in many areas, even academic ones like writing and arithmetic, children can learn in a self-regulated fashion. Cognitive learning is as natural, spontaneous, and important for children as is their social-emotional development.

The next example sheds more light on the child's self-directed learning and on the role of the parent. The episode (parts of which we have already reviewed in Chapter 1) concerns Deborah and Rebecca, at age 4–11, learning to say the counting numbers, and begins with some self-imposed practice.

D: 1, 2, 1, 2, 1, 2.

R: 1, 2, 3.

D: No, not like that. I said, 1, 2, 1, 2, 1, 2.

R: 1, 2, 3, 4, 5, 6, 7, 8.

D: 1, 2, 3, 4, 5, 6, 7, 8, 9, 10, 11, 12, 13, 14, 15, 16, 17, 18, 19.

Soon Rebecca decided to explore more difficult problems. Rebecca asked her mother, "What's after 19?"

M: 20.

R: 20, 21, 22, 23, 24, 25, 26, 27, 28, 29. What's after?

M: 30.

R: 31, 32, 33, 34, 35, 36, 37, 38. 39. Now 40.

M: Good.

R: 41, 42, 43, 44, 45, 46, 47, 48, 49 [pause] 50.

M: Good.

R: 51, 52, 53, 54, 55, 56, 57, 58, 59.

Here Rebecca paused and looked at her mother, apparently in search of the next number.

M: 60.

The counting continued for a while and eventually Rebecca was able to do "40, 50, 60, 70, 80, 90, tenny."

The episode illustrates two points we have already reviewed: children practice on their own and attempt moderately difficult problems when they could simply repeat what is easy. The episode also shows that children use the adult as a resource, as a source of information. Rebecca asked for information only at difficult points. She learned from the adult when she needed to, and not simply when the adult decided that she must learn.

So children's learning is self-directed in the sense that:

Children choose to be interested in certain topics.

Children decide to practice at certain times.

Children attempt to expand their knowledge.

Children request information when they believe it is needed.

If learning is self-directed, what then is the role of the parent and the culture? Do children learn entirely on their own? No. Arithmetic, like language, is very much a cultural product. It is not transmitted through the genes. Rather, basic aspects of arithmetic, like the decimal system of counting, are passed down through a process of learning, from generation to generation. Children profit from this legacy of culture: they do not have to recreate the entire body of arithmetic by themselves. Through the parents, through books and television, culture provides children with wisdom they can use; they do not learn solely on their own.

But learning is more than training. While children are heavily dependent on the culture for both guidance and information—for example, they cannot count without knowing the names of the counting numbers—there is a certain sense in which they themselves control the process of learning: they decide what they are interested in learning, when to practice, when to ask for information. They assimilate the cultural legacy into their own frame of reference, as when, for example, they think that "five" refers only to five blue objects or when they do arithmetic by finger counting.

Piaget uses the terms *assimilation* and *accommodation* to describe this process. On the one hand, children assimilate into their own understanding what culture has to offer: thus, they interpret "three" as a triangular shape. On the other hand, they accommodate themselves to the cultural wisdom: they try to learn the counting numbers in their conventional form. There is always a tension—a delicate balance—between the individual's contribution and the culture's.

SUMMARY

Part of children's motivation for learning arithmetic is practical utility. They learn to count or add because these techniques are useful for playing games, or going to the store, or telling time. In some societies without schooling, practical necessity motivates individuals to learn many arithmetic skills. Another source of motivation is intrinsic to arithmetic activity. Children learn to count or add because these activities are interesting in themselves. Such motivation can be very powerful and can take unexpected forms, as when some children find drilling by rote a fascinating endeavor.

There is a certain sense in which children's learning is self-directed. They practice tasks that interest them and they attempt moderately difficult problems when simpler ones are possible. Also, they seem to ask for help when it is needed. At the same time, their learning depends on cultural contributions. Arithmetic is a cultural legacy and people help children to learn it. In children's learning of arithmetic, there is always a balance between the personal and the cultural. Children assimilate the cultural contribution into their own framework; at the same time, they accommodate their thought to the cultural wisdom.

PRINCIPLES

1. *In the natural environment, children are spontaneously interested in cognitive learning.* Without the benefit of instruction, children spontaneously attempt to learn simple arithmetic, just as they naturally learn language or how to deal with people. Intellectual development is entirely normal and does not need forcing; children even enjoy it. Intellectual development is as central to children's lives as is their social-emotional development.

2. *Several kinds of motivation operate simultaneously in young children and may assume unexpected forms.* Children learn arithmetic (and other things) for many reasons. One is that arithmetic is useful in one way or another in the natural environment. Another is that such learning is fun in itself. Surely there are other kinds of motivation as well, like pleasing an adult. There is no one reason for learning arithmetic, just as there is no one reason for going to a concert. Sometimes children even manage to find interest in apparently dull drill.

3. *Young children make a significant contribution to their own learning.* Despite the necessity for an adult or cultural contribution, children control their own learning in significant ways. They choose to be interested in certain topics; they practice; they attempt moderately difficult problems; and they seek information under certain circumstances.

PRACTICAL ARITHMETIC

Young children can count; they have intuitions about number; and they can learn on their own. At four or five years of age they begin to combine the technology of counting with their mathematical ideas. The result is a practical arithmetic—means for dealing informally with real world mathematical problems. This practical arithmetic continues in use throughout the early school years and even beyond.

Addition and subtraction by counting

The environment, pervaded as it is with quantity, often presents children with practical arithmetic problems. The child ate two candies before; she eats three now; and her mother wants to know how many she has had altogether. (Later in school, word problems attempt to simulate realistic situations like these.) What do children do when faced with problems that we would solve by addition or subtraction? They cannot take refuge in a fear of mathematics: these are real life problems, not school exercises.

Children's solutions involve at least these two steps. First, they have to *interpret* the problem; they have to decide what kind of problem it is and which of their intuitions apply to the problem. Is it necessary to put things together or to take things away? Second, they have to *implement* what they have decided to do. If they think the problem involves combining, they have to put together 2 and 3 to determine the sum. If they think it is necessary to remove things, then that is what they must do: they have to take away 2 from 3 to see how many remain.

Adults find simple problems of this sort exceedingly trivial and often cannot imagine why children have difficulty with them. But as we have seen, children's thought may be different from ours and hence their interpretation of the problem may not be the same as our own. Also, they may have trouble in implementing a solution since they lack a simple method for doing the arithmetic that has been decided on. At four or five years, they do not know the addition facts and so cannot just remember, as we do, the sum of 2 and 3.

Suppose that children are presented with 2 blocks at the left and 3 at the right and are asked how many there are altogether. In a situation like this, most three-year-olds do not interpret the problem correctly. They apparently do not even realize that the answer can be obtained by combining the sets (in reality or by counting), and therefore do not attempt to count them. By about four years of age, some children—but not all—interpret the problem correctly and try to achieve a solution by counting the objects one by one, although they are not always successful. By about five years of age, virtually all children have no difficulty interpreting the problem. They usually solve it by some form of counting—for example, counting on from the larger number (that is, start with 3, the value of the larger set, and count on two more). This is reminiscent of the trend toward efficiency and economy in children's efforts to determine the number of elements in single collections.[10]

But practical arithmetic involves more than combining and counting. It involves several intellectual processes.[11] Vivian was shown one plate with three toy mice on it, and another plate with 5. The plates were hidden and the interviewer surreptitiously removed two mice from the five mice plate, so that both plates now had 3. The question was: how would Vivian interpret the secret subtraction of two mice? She saw first that one plate had 3; then she looked at the other.

V: Wait. There's 1—2—3. It has 3.

I: What happened?

V: Must have disappeared.

I: What?

V: The other mouses.

I: Where did they disappear from?

V: One was here and one was here. There was one there, one there, one there, one there, one there. This one is three now but before it was five.

I: What would you need to fix it?

V: I'm not really sure because my brother is real big and he could tell.

I: What do you think he would need?

V: Well I don't know. . . . Some things have to come back.

I: [The interviewer gave Vivian some objects including four mice.]

V: [Vivian put all four mice on the plate.] There. Now there's 1, 2, 3, 4, 5, 6, 7. No, I'll take these off [she pointed to two] and we'll see how many.

After a bit of clumsiness, she finally removed two to get the desired five.

Vivian's approach to this apparently simple task was complex, illustrating several intellectual processes. First, she *remembered* that the plates she had seen contained three and five respectively. She saw that there were fewer toys on one plate than there had been before—some mice had "disappeared." She knew *how many* had disappeared. She knew that the subtraction could be undone by an addition—that is, she understood something of the *relationship between addition and subtraction*. And finally, she *counted* to perform the necessary addition.

Suppose that children are asked to add *imaginary* objects: how many are three cows and two cows? Now children cannot simply count objects that they can see in front of them. Instead they have to represent the imaginary objects. They have to use concrete objects, or tallies, or mental "pictures" to stand for the imaginary objects. The children must then perform the arithmetic operations on the surrogates, the representations, not on the real things.

Some children are remarkably precocious in the addition of imaginary objects. Court reports that at three years her son enjoyed story problems like this:

" 'There is one nest on the top of a tree and one nest on a lower branch. How many nests do you think you can find on that tree?' He would then make a 'nest' with each of his little hands, would place them one above the other, and would find the answer."[12]

So Paul made a hand stand for, or represent, a nest, and by thus converting the story into concrete form was able to solve the problem, at least when small numbers were involved.

Eventually, children develop greater proficiency at adding larger numbers of imaginary objects. Ronnie, a second grader, was asked to add nine and three imaginary dots. He started to count aloud, "One, two, three," but then seemed uncomfortable and looked around. He needed concrete objects to count. The only object available was the microphone used for recording. Pointing to parts of the microphone, Ronnie began with four and counted on nine more, to get the correct answer, 13. He had transformed the microphone into a collection of objects to count.

One common aid to counting is the fingers, although at first children make mistakes in using them.

At 5–8, Rebecca was asked, "How much is 5 and 6?"

R: 5 and 6? I don't know.

I: Can you figure it out?

Rebecca began by counting the fingers on each hand. "1, 2, 3, 4, 5." She got 10 as the result.

I: No, I said, 5 and 6.

Again Rebecca counted the fingers on each hand, touching each one to her mouth as she called its number. Again she got 10 as the answer. She could not figure out a way of representing 5 and 6 on her fingers at the same time. Obviously, when the sum is greater than 10, finger counting demands special techniques—methods of which Rebecca was not yet capable.

Another child was more adept at finger counting. Asked how

she would add nine and six imaginary dots, Kathy, a lively second grader, first indicated a preference for counting real objects, but then said she would use her fingers.

K: I would draw a box and put the dots in and count them.

I: Know any other ways?

K: Well, I could count by my fingers, like 9, 10, 11, 12, 13, 14, 15.

I: And you think that will give you the total number of dots in the boxes?

K: Yes. 'Cause I used the biggest number first so I don't have to count as much.

So Kathy used a very efficient form of finger counting: counting on from the larger number.

A similar procedure is used for subtraction. At 7–3, Rebecca was asked, "How much is twelve take away five?"

R: 13, 14. No, wait. 12, 11, 10, 9, 8, 7.

Mathematics and Concrete Experience

Children's mathematics seems to grow from concrete experiences with objects. Children see that this *object* is bigger than that *object,* or that three *things* and two *things* make five *things*. Children's mathematics is in many ways concrete. But real mathematics is abstract and transcends physical reality: "bigger than" is an idea that is not limited to concrete objects; and 3 and 2 is still 5 without things. Mathematics itself concerns relations among ideas, not real objects (although it may be applied to real objects). Should one therefore conclude that children's mathematics should be discouraged? While in many senses "concrete," children's mathematics is a necessary first step in the direction of abstraction. Children's abstract ideas develop from their concrete experience. This leads to an educational paradox: abstract ideas can seldom be taught directly; they need to emerge from concrete experience.

This is a very old idea. In 1842, the educator Colburn, a follower of Pestalozzi, wrote: "The idea of number is first acquired by observing sensible objects. . . . We first make calculations about sensible objects; and we soon discover the same calculations will apply to things very dissimilar; and finally that they can be made without reference to any particular thing."[13]

As she said this, she pointed to her fingers.

Other children begin to internalize the process of counting: they no longer need to use the fingers and can count in their heads. Chris, a second grader, gives a graphic example of this. Asked how he solved an addition problem, he said, "I counted it up in my mind."

I: Now I have to know how you counted it up in your mind.

C: I put a picture in my mind saying, one finger's up, two fingers up, three fingers up, four fingers up, then five fingers up. And then I counted up to nine; I kept on counting to nine.

In describing how she counted in her head, Theresa, also a second grader, gives insight into the mysteries of the mind. "There's a reason that you can count in your head by your own words. . . . My counting would be going in my head and my mouth wouldn't be talking."

Eventually children become proficient at both addition and subtraction by counting.

Danny, at age 7–6, was given this problem.

I: It's eighty degrees now, and it was fifty degrees last week. How much colder was last week than this week?

D: I'd have to count. Count backwards.

I: Don't you think there is an easier way to do it?

D: Count from 50 to 80.

So, when asked to find a difference, Danny persisted in counting despite the interviewer's implied objection. Furthermore, he recognized, at least on an implicit level, the equivalence between forward and backward counting.

Written aids

We have seen how children can use surrogate objects, fingers, or even mental representations to solve arithmetic problems involving imaginary objects. Yet children's practical arithmetic suffers from a major limitation: it is overly dependent on memory. In adding two imaginary groups of objects, children have to remember how many are in both the first and the second. They also have to remember how many of each group have been counted. And if they want to check their computations there is no permanent record of what they have done, so that they have to start all over from the beginning.

There is one simple solution to the problem of memory: one can keep written records. These records offer the advantage of transforming events over time into a static, visual "picture" or array that does away with the need for memory.

While writing can be a powerful cognitive tool, the question now is whether children spontaneously use it, and how. When pencil and paper are available, how do children use them in the service of their practical arithmetic? During the preschool years, when children are generally incapable of making written numbers or words, do they use tallies or other forms of written symbolism to deal with arithmetic problems? During the early school years, when children learn written number, do they use it in the service of calculation?

We shall see that written work presents special difficulties. Even when children possess a powerful practical arithmetic, they are not adept at employing the most elementary forms of written symbolism such as the tally.

At age 5, Rebecca could easily count and add reasonable numbers of concrete objects. Yet, when asked to use tallies, she could not even represent a group of objects before her. In this situation, she struggled with the entire process: she sometimes counted the objects incorrectly; she sometimes found it hard to produce one and only one tally for each object. For her, written symbolism was more of a burden than an aid.

It was even more difficult for her to use tallies for the purpose of addition. Given this task, she made many errors in representing the members of each collection. There was much erasing and starting again. When she finally did manage to represent the members of each set, she failed to count the total properly. Given all these difficulties, it is no wonder that so few young children spontaneously use tallies or other forms of written symbolism to solve practical arithmetic problems.[14]

In brief, there is a gap, a discontinuity between children's practical arithmetic and their ability to do written arithmetic, even when this involves only tallies. Young children can solve problems by counting on fingers or in the head, but not by making marks on paper. For adults, tallies make calculation easier; for children, tallies make it harder. Why should this be so?

One reason may be that tally-making presents children with an extra task requiring more attention and effort than they are capable of. Not only do they have to count a set of objects, they also have to produce a like set of tallies. The work is at least doubled, and perhaps this is too much for them.

A second reason is that mathematical events are by their very nature hard to represent on paper. For example, addition is a dynamic process, taking place over time. We have 3 things now, then we add 2 things, and the result is 5 things. A motion picture would better represent this series of events over time than would a few marks on the static, two-dimensional surface of a piece of paper. Adults can use standard arithmetic symbolism to represent events like these. Thus, we write 3 + 2 = 5, where the + can be interpreted as referring to adding over time. But little children do not know these symbols. Can they use other means for "picturing" the actions of addition or subtraction?

Allardice[15] has done the most (and perhaps only) interesting study in this area. She finds that at first it is very hard for young children to represent on paper the operations or events of arithmetic. In the case of addition, she gave four and five year old children the following situation. A toy frog is on the table; after a period of time, two more toy frogs come along to join him; the result is three toy frogs. The children could easily describe the situation in *words*; they knew perfectly well that there was one frog at the outset and that two more frogs came along. But they did not put this on paper: they simply represented the final result and lost track of everything else. For example, a child might simply draw three tallies, grouped together, to represent the entire sequence of actions. They were not able to produce representation like this:

$$| + \| \rightarrow \|| \qquad \text{or even} \qquad | \quad \| \quad \||.$$

Allardice showed that children have particular difficulty in representing on paper the order of events. Young children were given a problem like this: "Here is a ball, and now here is a cat, and now here is a pencil. I want you to put something on paper that will show your friends which one I showed you first, which one I showed you next, and which one I showed you after that." Children managed to draw each of the three things so that there was a record of what they saw. And indeed they first drew the first object shown them, next the second object, and so on. The only problem was that these objects were placed randomly on the paper so that the order was not preserved for a viewer.

From about five to seven years of age, children gradually acquire skill at using tallies and other forms of written symbolism to keep track of the number of a collection, and the order of events. At 5 years of age, Rob was asked how many dogs there would be if he began with four and then got three more. He carefully put down four dots with a 4 above them, and then in a separate group, three dots with a 3 above them. He then counted the number of dots altogether, to get seven, and entirely ignored the numerals. For him, the dots, not the numerals, were the relevant symbols by which one could calculate.[16]

Here is another example of the use of symbols for calculation. Liam, at 6–2, was given the following problem by the interviewer, his mother.[17]

I: Let's pretend it is your birthday. We have invited twelve children, but all we have is seven cups to put the candies in. How many more cups do we have to buy? You can figure it out anyway you want. Use the paper and pencil, the M & M's [which were on the table], or anything else.

L: [Liam drew twelve circles, counting them. See Figure 3–1.]

$$\text{O O O O O O O O O O O O}$$

Figure 3–1. *Liam's circles*

I: How many do you have there?

L: [He underlined each circle as he counted it. Then he drew a continuous line under all twelve circles.] Twelve.

I: Twelve what?

L: Twelve children.

I: Right, and we have seven cups. How are we going to figure out how many cups we need?

L: [He drew seven more circles, counting each as he drew it.]

I: O.K. So we have twelve children and seven cups. If you give out all the cups, some kids still won't have any. How can you show what will happen on the paper?

L: [He thought for a few seconds.] Should I draw a line to each one?

I: Why don't you try it?

L: [He drew a curved line, as in Figure 3–2, from each "cup" to a "child," then he connected the circles left over.] Five, you need five more cups!

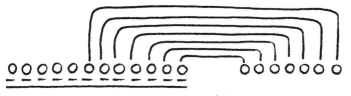

Figure 3–2. *Liam's solution*

Liam's behavior has several interesting features. First, he used symbols as a calculating machine. Drawing lines from "cups" to "children" was a device for subtracting. Second, as Kennedy points out, "The values of the symbols are interchanged easily. The circle represents either a cup or a child." In fact, the five circles on the extreme left initially represented children and then cups. Third, Liam did not bother to use written numbers, which he knew, to solve the problem; tallies were more meaningful.

Here is another example of how elementary symbols can be used for calculation. Bob was asked, "If you had four people and you wanted to give seven pennies to each one of them, how many pennies would you have to have altogether?"[18] Bob solved this multiplication problem by drawing tallies as follows:

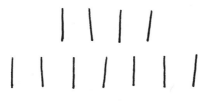

Figure 3–3. *Bob's multiplication machine*

He counted the bottom row of seven tallies four times. Each time he did so, he kept track of his action by crossing out one of the tallies in the top row of four. In effect, he had constructed a simple multiplication machine which for him was more powerful than writing down $4 \times 7 = $.

Let us now return to the problem Liam solved—seven cups for twelve children—by means of elementary symbols. By contrast, Liam's friend James (5–7) tried to use formal symbols. Given the same problem, he quickly answered "two."

I: Can you work it out in the same way [motioning to the paper, pencil, and M & M's]?

J: [He wrote on the paper: 7. cups AND, 12.] How do you spell children?

I: C-h-i-l-d-r-e-n.

J: [He wrote, CHILDREN AD 2 cups] One, two, three, four, five, six, seven—Oh!—eight, nine, ten, eleven, twelve [He erased *AD 2 cups* and wrote instead: *8 9 10 112 13 14 15*. Then he erased *13 14 15* and wrote in *cups* instead. See Figure 3–3.]

J: Eight, nine, ten, eleven, twelve are missing cups.

I: So, now how many more cups should your mommy buy?

J: She should buy eight, nine, ten, eleven, twelve cups.

I: But how many cups is that?

J: It's eight, nine, ten, eleven, twelve.

I: How many children need cups?

J: Eight, nine, ten, eleven, twelve.

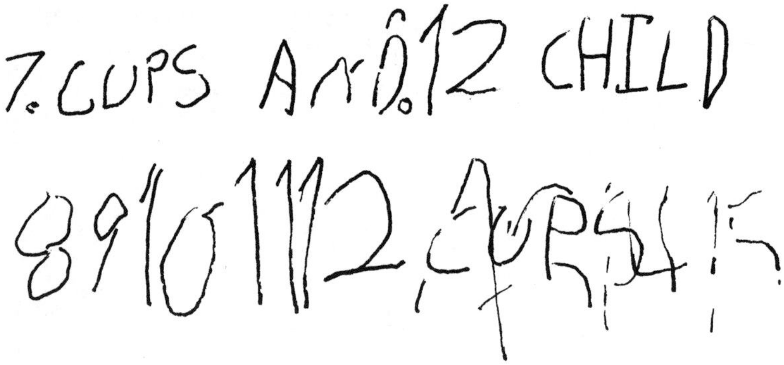

Figure 3–4. *James's solution*

We see then that although James was able to produce written numbers, he did not know how to use them to solve the problem. Instead of counting the children labelled eight, nine, ten, eleven, twelve to get the number of cups required, he simply repeated the children's number *names*. He said, in effect, "Jacky, Johnny, and Jimmy need cups," instead of determining that Jacky, Johnny, and Jimmy are three children so that three cups are required. (Recall the case of Moira who believed that if she ate piece of bread number one, three still remained, because two and three were uneaten.) So by focussing on mere labels, James wasted the power of his advanced technology—written number. As Kennedy puts it, his "competence in writing numbers exceeds his genuine understanding."[19]

It is ironic that Liam and Bob were able to achieve an accurate solution by far simpler means. Both used simple tallies in a genuinely *symbolic* manner: Liam's circles stood for children and then for the missing cups. James used symbols in a genuinely *concrete* manner: his written numerals were mere names. Once again, we see that language—here written numbers—is but a poor guide to thought.

Characteristics of practical arithmetic

Children's practical arithmetic—the addition and subtraction they develop before school instruction—displays some important characteristics: children are comfortable with it; it is extremely widespread, if not universal; and it can be powerful.

Young children are quite comfortable with informal arithmetic. Faced with a practical arithmetic problem in their natural surroundings—for example, how much money is needed to buy a five cent piece of candy and a ten cent piece—children usually solve it by counting on their fingers. This is a safe, familiar procedure, arousing no particular anxiety. Children seem relaxed with finger counting; it is a trusted tool. (One hears that even adults occasionally resort to finger counting when all else fails.)

Why is informal arithmetic so comfortable and easy while school arithmetic is so often fraught with anxiety? One reason may be that informal arithmetic develops in a relatively "natural" way in the child's ordinary environment. Just as children learn to speak, so they learn to do practical arithmetic. In both cases, they can learn only if they get some basic information from adults (the words of the language and the counting numbers); but they do not require formal instruction. Also, in both cases they undertake much of the learning on their own initiative, and they learn because *they* find it useful and enjoyable to learn, not because someone else does.

Informal arithmetic is extremely widespread. In Western cultures, children use it both before and after entering school. They do arithmetic by counting, generally finger counting, regardless of the kind of instruction they are subjected to in the early grades of school. This is a fact that can be documented with the greatest of ease by virtually any parent or teacher.

Indeed, informal arithmetic can be found all around the world. According to Conant:

> The one primitive method of counting which seems to have been almost universal throughout all times is the finger method. It is a matter of common experience and observation that every child when he begins to count, turns instinctively to his fingers; and with these convenient aids as counters, tallies off the little number he has in mind.

This method is at once so natural and obvious that there can be no doubt that it has always been employed by savage tribes, since the first appearance of the human race in remote antiquity. All research among civilized peoples has tended to confirm this view, were confirmation needed of anything so patent.[20]

While Conant perhaps exaggerates his position, it is clear that some "primitive" cultures have developed rather elaborate systems of arithmetic based almost entirely on counting. In rural India, illiterate persons use a variety of finger counting methods to deal effectively with money lenders and shopkeepers.[21] In the Ivory Coast, illiterate Dioula tribesmen use counting-based procedures to perform addition in the market place.

Not only is arithmetic by counting extremely widespread, it has a long and distinguished history. According to Dantzig:

Only a few hundred years ago finger counting was such a widespread custom in Western Europe that no manual of arithmetic was complete unless it gave full instructions in the method. The art of using his fingers in counting and in performing the simple operations of arithmetic was then one of the accomplishments of an educated man.[22]

How powerful is practical arithmetic? As practiced by most children in Western cultures, practical arithmetic, especially finger counting, is adequate for the solution of addition and subtraction problems involving relatively small numbers, like 23 + 18 or 87 + 16. The method is only infrequently used with multiplication when the latter involves relatively small numbers and is interpreted as repeated addition (thus, 4 × 8 is taken as 8 + 8 + 8 + 8 and

---

Abacus Whips Calculator!

According to the *Wall Street Journal*,[23] a prominent mathematical publication, there is still hope for informal methods of calculation. A competition was held between a United States calculator executive and an Oriental businessman using the ancient abacus. While the American poked around trying to find the plus button, the Oriental smoothly manipulated the wooden beans and water buffalo horn pegs. It was no contest; the abacus was quicker almost every time.

solved by counting). In our culture, then, informal arithmetic is of relatively limited scope. Even so, it can be used for ordinary shopping, which typically requires addition as the main operation.

In other cultures, informal arithmetic is used to greater effect. As already mentioned, tribesmen in Africa use informal arithmetic, including multiplication, for complex commercial activities. As Dantzig observed, the same was true in Western Europe several centuries ago. Indeed, history shows that effective finger methods have been developed for dealing with multiplication and with very large numbers—in one system, up to 9,000.[24]

Informal arithmetic by counting can be useful and powerful: we should help children to perfect their technique.

SUMMARY

In the natural environment, children are frequently faced with problems that adults can solve by means of written arithmetic. Lacking this, children develop from their intuition and their counting skills a practical arithmetic. This involves at least two steps: the interpretation of problems and the implementation of a solution. Given concrete objects to add, three-year-olds do not interpret the problem correctly: they do not even realize that it is necessary to combine the objects in some way. By four years of age, the spirit is willing but the flesh is weak: many children realize that things must be combined but are not always good at doing the necessary counting. By five years of age, the problem presents no difficulty and children even use shortcuts like counting on from the larger number. Children also develop proficiency in dealing with imaginary objects. At first, the attempted solution is to represent the imaginary objects by real things and then count them up. Another solution is finger counting. Cross-cultural research shows that counting methods are extremely widespread, and history shows that they have taken elaborate and effective forms; indeed, finger counting was once considered the mark of an educated man. Eventually, children may bypass finger counting and carry out counting operations on a mental level. They also learn to use elementary methods of written symbolism, like tallying.

Children are quite comfortable with their self-developed practical arithmetic. Such procedures are extremely widespread, and can be used in relatively powerful ways.

PRINCIPLES

1. *Before entrance to school, children engage in arithmetic problem solving of an elementary nature.* In the natural environment, children develop informal ways of dealing with problems of addition, subtraction, and perhaps multiplication. It is not true that schooling introduces children to arithmetic; their practical, nonwritten arithmetic originates earlier.

2. *Counting forms the core of children's practical arithmetic.* Children add and subtract by counting, often on their fingers. Their practical arithmetic depends on counting as its basic computational technique.

3. *Written work presents special difficulties.* Children find it hard to represent on paper collections of objects and especially events over time. Children have difficulty in using even so elementary a device as the tally. It is easier for them to calculate on fingers or in the head than on paper.

Chapter 4

Helping Young Children

In this chapter, I offer ten suggestions on how to help young children, particularly preschool children, to learn elements of arithmetic.

1. Keep a proper balance between teaching and the fostering of spontaneous growth.

Helping preschool children requires maintaining perspective on the adult role. You should feel a certain modesty concerning what you can and cannot do. On the one hand, there are some important ways in which you can foster children's learning. You can provide them with a stimulating environment; you can respond to their interests and inquiries; you can correct some of their mistakes. All these activities (which will be considered in greater depth later in this chapter) can serve to enrich children's intellectual life. On the other hand, adult intervention can be irrelevant or even hurt children. In some ways, children's learning is robust: they develop certain quantitative concepts, like "more," without the adult's awareness, let alone assistance. You are simply not needed to help with these things. Conversely, in other ways, young children's thought is so immature that nothing much can be done to advance it. You cannot teach conservation, let alone calculus, to very little children. Try as you may, you cannot help with certain things. Furthermore, if you try too hard, the resulting pressure can be noxious. There is no point in pushing and pressuring young children. The main outcome is likely to be the destruction of their natural interest in mathematics.

In brief, there are certain ways in which you can help. Yet remember that in some areas children need no help; in other areas it does no good; and too much of it can be destructive.

2. Get acquainted with children's intellectual life.

The first step in helping children is getting to know what they are really up to. You must always keep in mind that children are continually engaged in attempts to understand their world. They are naturally curious. They try to figure out what comes after 20 and why; or what makes things bounce; or why people get mad. The adult often fails to recognize the true intellectual nature of children's activities because they appear so mundane and casual. Children's efforts at understanding are often manifested in make-believe counting while they are playing store; or in dropping a ball from different heights; or in arranging blocks in piles. It is easy for the adult to forget that significant intellectual work does not occur only in school, under adult supervision. Remember that play is children's work and that their intellectual life is extraordinarily rich. Whether or not you can help, you may have great pleasure in gaining insight into children's learning.

Sometimes you may find it easy to discern what children are trying to understand. Some of their concerns are immediately evident in their overt behavior—as when they try to say the numbers from "one" to "ten"—and recognizing these concerns requires no special powers of perception or analysis. But other intellectual struggles of children are not so obvious, as when they are engaged in learning how physical arrangements affect number. In these cases, to appreciate the meaning of children's activities you need to devote close attention to those activities despite their often trivial appearance. You need to observe closely what children do; you need to ask yourself what each act means. This is hard, but the effort is worthwhile, since to understand children's intellectual life is to know them more fully.

In trying to know children, you should be especially sensitive to their errors. We have seen that errors are seldom if ever trivial or meaningless; most often they reflect serious attempts to understand and are products of sensible approaches to a problem. You should not invariably dismiss errors as silly or thoughtless: they can provide useful insight into children's intellectual concerns. Indeed, you should devote special attention to children's errors.

The interpretation of errors is a pursuit with which we are quite familiar, at least in the realms of social and emotional behavior. In those areas we continually try to tease out the deeper meanings behind overt actions. We assume, for example, that children's bedwetting is not just an accident but is rather a reflection of an underlying and significant conflict. We all know that reasoning of this type is often quite useful. Now you must carry it one step further: realize that the children's ordinary behavior can yield insights into a deeper intellectual life too.

There are no easy formulas, no mechanical techniques that can guarantee sharp and accurate perception of children's thought. Observe their natural behavior and try to see what sense it makes. This is a creative activity that perhaps cannot easily be taught. Talk to them informally about the activities they spontaneously engage in: they may tell you what they are trying to do. But beware of children's words. They may not mean what they seem to mean. The child's "five" is not yours; you have to look below the surface to see what "five" really means.

Above all, recognize that children's arithmetic may be different from yours. For them, "more" can be "greater area"; for you it means the "more numerous." Don't expect their intellectual lives to be the same as those you are familiar with.

3. Make available to children a stimulating environment.

One way to help children is to provide them with a rich environment that can nourish their interests. We have seen that children are naturally curious; they are eager to learn. But they cannot invent the counting numbers for themselves; they cannot develop a practical arithmetic completely on their own. Children need a world of number from which they can learn. To discover the rules underlying the counting numbers, they need to hear them over and over again. To develop practical techniques for adding, they need to live in an environment where adding is appropriate and where it gets them something.

As Piaget has observed, intellectual growth occurs only in interaction with the environment. There is a real sense in which the environment provides food for thought.

But what kind of environment, what kind of intellectual food, do children need? It is sometimes useful to introduce specially designed experiences and materials. Young children can learn something about number from Sesame Street, from books, from educational toys, from nursery rhymes, from written numerals posted on the walls. All these things can be useful, although some are expensive. The general rule should be to enrich the environment as much as you can afford and as much as the children seem to enjoy.

At the same time do not forget that the natural environment itself—that is, the environment without specially designed games and toys—affords many opportunities for mathematical learning. In all environments, all cultures, there are things to count; collections are added and others are taken away; some things are bigger than others; and adults say the counting numbers. If children are involved in learning to count things, then mere pebbles may fit their needs exactly, whereas an expensive toy designed to teach mathematics readiness may miss the mark. No matter how impoverished the environment is in other ways, it can always provide at least a minimum level of stimulation with respect to quantity.

So exploit the ordinary environment in which children live. Recognize that fancy educational toys are not necessary; children can learn instead from card games and sticks and shopping.

The truth of this statement is shown by an African chief's account of mathematics learning in his tribe:

> The knowledge of numerals among the Yoruba people is as old as life itself. It is usually taught or imparted in different forms from childhood or as soon as a child can recognize an object. Pebbles, beans or stones are sometimes used in the teaching of numbers through demonstration. This teaching is also continued through traditional games . . . and often sharpens one's mental capacity for calculations. Children also learn the art of buying and selling while in company of their mothers at the market. Apart from helping with the supervised sales of the parent's articles, the children are also given a few wares of their own so as to give them confidence and as a test of their understanding of money values. The teaching could also be formal and informal, indoors and outdoors, and takes many forms.[1]

Finally, do not forget that aspects of the environment are stimulating only insofar as they meet the children's needs. Pebbles, books, and educational toys are not stimulating in themselves; they can help if and only if children can use them at a particular time in their development to satisfy their curiosity or learn something they want to know. There is a kind of relativity principle here: stimulation exists only in interaction with children's intellectual interests. If children are interested in counting things, then the pebbles that they have ignored all their lives may assume immense importance. When they are no longer concerned with counting, then the pebbles are no longer effective stimulants. This means that you need to match the stimulation you can offer—games, stories, whatever—to children's intellectual concerns.

4. Trust and support children's intellectual work.

Children are continually engaged in learning. They learn because they are intrinisically motivated to learn and because it is useful to do so. Their learning centers on important topics: they want to learn about space, time, and causality, life and death; they want to learn about the world of quantity. To a large extent, they can regulate their own learning: they learn a good deal on their own, without adult assistance. There is wide individual variability. Different children learn different things at different times. But all learn certain basic ideas and ways of seeing the world: there are intellectual universals, including certain mathematical ideas. All children learn about more and less, and about elementary equivalence. Before school, children develop mathematical ideas and are not afraid of them.

One contribution you can make to young children's intellectual work is to support it. Recognize that they have valid interests and try to nourish them. You do not need to make a choice between children's intellectual growth and their social-emotional development. Intellectual concerns are entirely natural to children, as natural as learning to walk or play with other children. The desire to learn counting can be as basic to the four-year-old as the desire to ride a bicycle. The four-year-old does not know what is intellectual and what isn't! And supporting children's intellectual work does not necessarily mean pushing or training or drilling. On the contrary, it can mean fostering just another variety of enjoyable play.*

So trust and support the child's spontaneous interests. They are serious and can lead to important intellectual growth.

5. Give special support to children's counting.

It is especially important to help children with their counting. There are several reasons for this. One is that counting in one form or another is likely to be their chief mathematical interest. Another is that counting is very basic to all of arithmetic: many problems in arithmetic can be solved by counting. And finally, it is in the area of counting that you are likely to do some good.

---

*I have heard of nursery schools that refuse to let the children learn to read and write on the grounds that such cognitive activity is an imposition and stunts social-emotional growth. The only imposition is in not letting the children learn what they want to learn. And the emotional outcomes are likely to be disappointment and boredom.

There are many specific ways in which you can help. When children are trying to learn the counting words, you can teach them the nursery rhymes for memorizing the first ten or so (meaningless) numbers. If they have trouble with the larger numbers—say from 10 to 100—you can try to focus their attention on the relevant rules. You can encourage the child to count by tens or to construct large numbers (like 400 or 500). This may lead them to see that very little rote learning is involved in counting; in general, the numbers can be constructed by rule.

On Rote Learning

Young children's meaningful learning of the counting words should make us wonder about the apparently "rote" nature of a good deal of arithmetic activity. If even so routine a process as learning to say the number words requires so little rote memory, then how much more so will this be true of other aspects of arithmetic? Given some basic ideas and counting skills, children in fact need to memorize very little. For example, if they can count, they can construct the addition or multiplication tables when required. The need for rote memory is greatly exaggerated. Children can avoid a lot of it by relying on their counting and creativity.

You can also help in children's counting of objects. They need repetitive practice in this. They need different things to count. You can help by counting with them and by pointing out when they are wrong. You can try to get them to see that each thing needs to be counted once and only once. You can help them to learn good strategies for doing this: teach them to push things aside after they have counted. They are likely to try to count on their fingers. Help them to do it. There is no harm in it.* After they have learned to count one by one, you can help them learn more efficient strategies. Show them how to group, how to count by twos and by fives.

You can also help children's practical arithmetic. They may be fascinated by how many things there are altogether when they combine two groups or take one away from the other. Give them simple arithmetic problems with real objects; they may enjoy the activity, as Court's son did. Show them how to add and subtract

*If it worries you, repeat fifty times a day: "In eighteenth century Europe, finger counting used to be the mark of an educated man or woman." Keep track of the repetitions by counting on your fingers.

on the fingers. After they have mastered that, perhaps they will enjoy calculating with tallies.

In the nursery school, don't be afraid of working with arithmetic directly. (As we shall see below, there is no need to be concerned with prearithmetic activities, with readiness.) There exist a number of interesting devices and materials appropriate to the four- and five-year levels: Cuisenaire rods, Stern Blocks, the abacus, Montessori materials. Any of these things can be useful for different children at different times. One child may find the Cuisenaire rods useful, another the abacus. There is no easy way of knowing what may work. Use whatever proves effective to foster children's spontaneous interests as they emerge.

Finally, here is a list of things to avoid.

6. Don't try to teach little children the new math.

Sets and logic make a certain amount of sense to some mathematicians, but this approach is virtually useless for young children. They need to learn to count and to add; sets and unions and equipollence are quite beside the point.

7. Avoid formal training, especially verbal instruction.

It seldom helps to train children in whatever it is you think they ought to learn. You cannot easily impose understanding on them. It is especially futile to give them a lot of verbal explanations. You can *tell* them to count one by one or that addition is counting forward on the number line; but this will help as little as telling them to ride a bicycle by first placing one foot there, and then. . . .

Training seldom works. Children need to learn in other ways. In Piaget's view, "real comprehension of a concept . . . implies its reinvention by the child. . . . It is important first that the child should have been able to find, by himself, the reasons for the truth that he is expected to understand, and second, that he should have at least partially reinvented it for himself. That naturally does not mean that the teacher [or parent] is useless, but his role ought to consist less in giving 'lessons' than in organizing situations provoking investigation."[2]

So try not to train and to instruct; try to foster and respond to children's attempts to learn.

8. Don't bother with readiness activities.

Some nursery school (and some elementary school) practice is based on the assumption that before children can learn arithmetic (or reading) directly, they must first engage in readiness activities of one kind or another. Readiness often consists of such activities as seeing that a circle is different from a square or that one line is longer than another. So far as I can tell, this seems to be almost a complete waste of time. These are things that children already know how to do, and in any event their relevance to arithmetic (or reading) is not at all clear. Children do not need to be made ready for elementary arithmetic (or reading): they are *already* interested and engaged in it.*

9. Don't waste time on the training of conservation.

Some Piagetian curricula try to teach children to conserve or to solve other Piagetian problems. This makes little sense on two grounds. One is that the Piagetian concepts are very hard to teach; the training usually does not work. The second reason is that all children spontaneously learn to conserve in due course, without adult assistance. Conservation is about the last thing they need help with. You can more profitably spend your time by helping children to pursue *their* interests, like finger counting.

Piagetian training is now a fad. But there is little sense to it. Piaget himself wonders why Americans find it so important to speed up the development of conservation.

10. Keep in mind preschool children's tremendous accomplishments.

By the age of five or six, children have learned an enormous amount. Upon their entrance to school, most children have the intellectual prerequisites for understanding the basic ideas of arithmetic taught there. Children understand more and less, they can count, they can add in a practical way, and perhaps they can

*Despite the popularity of the Frostig materials, the same is true of reading. Before school, four-and five-year-olds spontaneously learn to discriminate among letters, to write them, and even to read a bit. They are already ready. See Gibson, E. J. and Levin, H. The *psychology of reading*. Cambridge, Mass.: MIT Press, 1975.

conserve. Don't focus just on children's weaknesses. Remember that there is a good deal they can do. According to Piaget, the arithmetic taught in school is but an extension or formalization of what children already know. Children's intuitions can form a solid basis for school learning.

Piaget says that "it is difficult to conceive how students who are well endowed when it comes to the elaboration and utilization of the spontaneous [patterns] of intelligence can find themselves handicapped in the comprehension of a branch of teaching [mathematics] that bears exclusively upon what is to be derived from such [thought]."[3] In other words, children typically develop powerful informal modes of thought, powerful intuitions. Given this equipment, they should not find it difficult to learn school arithmetic, since the latter is merely a formalization and extension of what they already know. By around age five or six, almost every child has the intellectual ability to learn basic mathematical ideas; this competence is what we should always keep in mind.

School Learning

We have seen that counting serves as a surprisingly effective basis for young children's informal arithmetic. Yet counting has its obvious limits, and is cumbersome to use for multiplication and division. Children can enrich their knowledge and technique by learning the arithmetic taught in school. Unlike their own, this arithmetic is *codified:* it is written, and arranged systematically, with explicit rules and procedures. Codified arithmetic allows the user to deal with imaginary mathematical objects, to remember what he or she has done, and to communicate the results to others. Codified arithmetic typically needs to be taught through a process of *formal* instruction; that is, in the classroom. Children cannot by themselves reinvent the symbols and methods of arithmetic. Written arithmetic is a cultural legacy: it represents the accumulated wisdom of the race, written down so as to be available to all, and is obviously far superior to children's informal arithmetic. At the same time, there is a great paradox here: while codified arithmetic is enormously powerful, few children find it useful. Part II of this book explores the paradox: it tries to show what and how children learn in school, and why they understand or fail to understand codified arithmetic.

Chapter 5

Computing with Written Numbers

School arithmetic is based on written numbers like 7 and 6 and on symbols like + and −. These tell you what numbers to use and what to do with them. Children must learn to write the symbols of arithmetic and to read them. They must also learn to understand them, and to use them properly in computation.

WRITING AND READING

Writing

Court's son Paul was, as we have seen, an enthusiastic and accomplished practical mathematician. At the age of 5–1, Paul could count by ones up to one million and by tens to 1,000; clearly knew which numbers were greater in magnitude than others; could add, using counters, up to 20; and could boast of many other arithmetic accomplishments. *Yet Paul could not write any symbols except 1.* Clearly, written work lags behind the child's informal mathematics.

Eventually, children develop an interest in written numbers. They see adults writing them, or they want to learn how to tell time, or to write down how old they are. Perhaps they encounter written numbers only on entering school and want to learn them there. In any event, they want to make on paper the marks that everyone agrees to be 4, 5, and the like.

Learning to write numbers is very much like learning to say them. At first, children have to memorize the first ten digits, from 0 to 9. These are completely arbitrary and must be learned by rote. There is no reason why 4 should stand for the spoken number "four," just as there is no reason why the first spoken number should be "one," not "five" or some arbitrary sound like "biv." So children have to learn, through a brute process, that 1 goes along with the spoken word "one," 2 with "two" and so on. Such learning is mechanical and dull, but eventually children do it, just as they learn to say "one, two, three . . . ten."

Numbers, Numerals and All That

Some find it useful to distinguish between numbers and numerals. Numerals are written symbols, whereas numbers are the ideas that the symbols stand for. So *4,* as written on paper, is the numeral, not the number itself; *4* is just a symbol, like the written *four* or the spoken word "four." These symbols stand for the abstract idea of four, the number itself. This nice distinction is not of earthshaking importance for children just learning their numbers. Here is what one child, nine years of age, thought of the whole business:

"I've come to the conclusion that these rich, beautiful people always call a number a numeral . . . it's more pleasant than number . . . that's the difference, I think. . . . But *I* don't know the difference between a number and a numeral. It doesn't make sense to me."[1]

But once children master the first ten digits, their learning can take on a different character. The written numbers after 9 are organized by place value. We write our numbers—like 2,232—so that a digit acquires its value by virtue of its left to right location. The 2 on the extreme right stands for 2 × 1; the 2 in the middle for 2 × 100; and the 2 on the left for 2 × 1,000. We could say the number as "two thousand, two hundred, and thirty (three tens) and two." We write the number in much shorter and more convenient form because we can drop out explicit reference to thousands and hundreds and merely represent these by left-right position. So just as the spoken number song after 12 or 13 makes sense, so does the written number song after 9.*

---

*From a technical point of view, the written number song is a better song. There are no exceptions at all. You write 11 and 21 and 31 according to the same principle. But you *say* "eleven" and "twenty-one," which do not operate by the same rule, although "twenty-one" and "thirty-one" do.

The Evolution of Written Number

As Dantzig puts it so well, "Written numeration is probably as old as private property." It may have developed when people, perhaps especially the rich, wanted to keep track of what they owned. The first written system, indicated number up to about 10 by a collection of strokes, and numbers after that by special symbols. For example, the Egyptians represented 2,876 by the arrangement shown in Figure 5–1. This system is fully capable of representing very large numbers, but is inflexible and does not permit easy computation. Systems like the Egyptian were the

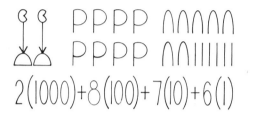

Figure 5–1. *The Egyptians' 2876*

only type available for thousand of years. Then somewhere around 100 or 200 A.D., the Indians invented the place value system in use today. Dantzig maintains that without place value no progress in arithmetic would have been possible. Indeed, he maintains that "achievement of the unknown Hindu who . . . discovered the *principle of position* assumes the proportions of a world-event."[2] Once the principle of position was developed, then algorithms like column addition became possible. These however did not become popular until about the eleventh century, since before then paper was very scarce in Europe.[3] Mathematical work on paper, with written numbers, is a very late historical development; before that time calculation was ordinarily done by machines like the abacus.

It takes several years for children to master the place value system for writing numbers. At the outset they sometimes make the error of writing numbers in the same way they say them. At 7–3, Rebecca was asked to write 23. She did *203*. Later she was asked to write 35 and wrote *305*. She often made mistakes of this type, writing, say, *402* for 42.

Rebecca had never been taught to write numbers in this fashion. Her errors, like her errors of spoken numbers, were obviously generated by a system of rules partly of her own invention. The (mistaken) rules mirror the spoken language. Since you *say* "forty-two" you write *402* as well.

Even after learning to write numerals properly four- and five-year-olds treat them in a somewhat cavalier fashion, as an interview by Allardice with Algie shows.[4]

> I: [Presents Algie with an array of 19 paper clips.] Can you put something on paper to show me how many there are?

Algie counted the clips one by one.

> A: Nineteen. But I can't write nineteen. So I'll put 11.

Another child who could not write 19 in this situation instead wrote all the numbers she *did* know. In general, if young children know what a certain quantity is, but do not know how to write it, they simply substitute some other number that they do know how to write!

Children soon master the conventional rules for writing small numbers, but they experience a difficulty similar to Rebecca's in the case of large numbers. Joe, eleven years of age, in grade five, was asked to write these numbers: 19; 472; 3; 6,023; 71,845; 56.[5]

Joe wrote:

$$19$$
$$472$$
$$3$$
$$600,023$$
$$710,00845$$
$$56$$

Joe knew the conventional rules for writing some numbers, namely those up to three digits (472). But after that point, he was stuck—he had not yet mastered the rules for numbers containing four digits (for example, 6,023) or more. When these were involved, Joe did essentially the same thing Rebecca did for smaller numbers. He wrote at least part of the number according to how it is spoken. Thus, for "six thousand twenty-three," he did *600,023*. This is again an example of a partly self-generated rule. It is also an example of a gap between children's approaches to big and small numbers. Children learn certain rules for small numbers but then, on encountering large ones, need to learn once more what are essentially the same rules. In a similar fashion, children who can do addition with two digit numbers need to learn it over again for three, even though the process is essentially the same in the two cases.

Reading

Reading numbers operates according to the same rules as writing them.

At 7–3, Rebecca was asked to read some numbers. The interviewer wrote 53.

R: Five and three. Eight.

I: No, I didn't say add them. Just read those two numbers.

R: Five and three.

So Rebecca read them as completely separate numbers, just as if she were asked to read *five, three.*

I: Can you read this now? [The interviewer wrote what Rebecca ordinarily wrote to express "fifty three," namely 503].

R: Fifty three.

Clearly Rebecca's rules for reading numbers were modelled on her rules for writing them. Of course, like the vast majority of children, she eventually learned the rules for both reading and writing numbers, up to a reasonable size. In fact, she went beyond what seemed reasonable. At eleven, she took great enjoyment in trying to read numbers into the zillions. One evening, in the best pizza restaurant in Ithaca, she, Deborah, and Jonathan insisted on playing a game that consisted of reading these steadily expanding numbers that the interviewer wrote on napkins:

$$1$$
$$12$$
$$123$$
$$1,234$$
$$12,345$$
$$123,456$$
$$1,234,567$$
$$12,345,678$$
$$123,456,789$$
$$1,234,567,890$$
$$12,345,678,901$$
$$\text{etc.}$$

They worked out the rules for reading numbers up through the trillions and stopped there only because the interviewer did not know what came next.

UNDERSTANDING

Children eventually learn to read and write elementary written symbolism but do not necessarily understand it in the same way we do.

+ and =

Suppose the child is shown some simple mathematical sentences. How does he interpret them? Kenneth, a first grader (about six or seven years), was shown the sentence $2 + 4 = \square$.[6]

> I: You read that [+], will you? What does that sign say?
>
> K: Plus.
>
> I: What does it tell you?
>
> K: It tells you to add this [2] and this [4].
>
> I: O.K. What can you tell me about that [=] symbol?
>
> K: Equals. That means, like this 2 plus this 4 equals 6. There has to be an equal there.

Kenneth interpreted + and = in terms of actions to be performed. So do other children. Presented with the same problem, Evelyn, also a first grader, maintained that $2 + 4 = \square$ means "to put number 6 in the box." She said that 2 and 4 are numbers but $2 + 4$ is not a number. A second grader, Donna, said that in $3 + 4 = \square$, "the = sign means what it adds up to."

The children's understanding of symbols refers to *actions*, to calculational operations. The form $a + b = \square$ means that you do something with $a + b$ to get a result, namely the sum.

This of course is one legitimate interpretation. In fact, most often when children are presented with sentences of that kind they are supposed to add up two numbers. Yet the interpretation is limited and can lead to trouble:

> I: How do you think you would read this [$\square = 3 + 4$]?
>
> K: . . . Blank equals 3 plus 4.
>
> I: O.K. What can you say about that, anything?
>
> K: It's backwards! [He changed it to $4 + 3 = \square$.] You can't go, 7 equals 3 plus 4.

Given the same problem, Tommy also changed it because, "it's backward," and asked the interviewer, "Do you read backwards?"

So one consequence of the child's interpretation in terms of action is that he finds it hard to read legitimate sentences that do not directly reflect the order of his calculations. The child first does 4 and then 3 to get 7, but that is not what the sentence says, so the sentence must be wrong.

The child's interpretation also leads him to distort some sentences. Kenneth was asked to read $\square = 2 + 5$. He said, in effect, that he had to switch around the $+$ and $=$ signs, because they were obviously in the wrong places. This results in "trying to add up to five," namely, $\square + 2 = 5$. Later, Kenneth was shown $3 = 5$.

I: What can you say about that?

K: Cross that line out. [Kenneth wrote over the $=$ sign to change it to $3 + 5$.]

I: Can I write this [$3 = 3$]? Does it make sense?

K: Nope. Now you could fix that by going like this. [He changed it to $0 + 3 = 3$.]

When Charles was shown $3 = 5$, he counted on his fingers and wrote $3 =_8 5$. "Five . . . there's no plus. That makes it wrong. I'll put a plus in the middle." He wrote $3 +_8 5$.

We see that if the child always interprets symbols in terms of actions on numbers, he cannot read sentences that express relationships, like $3 = 3$ or $4 = 4$.

What is the reason for children's tendency to interpret symbols in terms of actions? I think that their interpretation may simply reflect the ordinary demands of the classroom. Most often, sentences *do* ask children to perform a calculation; if so, why should they interpret them otherwise?

Is 31 the same as 13?

Eventually children succeed at reading and writing individual numbers of reasonable size, like 234. But do they *understand* why numbers are written as they are? Why can't you write "two hundred thirty four" as 432? Our question then is to what extent do children explicitly understand the rationale for writing numbers—the idea of place value? I have found it useful to distinguish among three stages in children's understanding of written number.

In *Stage I*, children can write a number correctly, but cannot explain the rationale for doing so at all. The case of Chris, in grade two, is illustrative.

Chris had just written that $9 + 5 = 14$.

I: Now I'm going to ask you something about 14. How come you wrote 14 with a 1 and then a 4?

C: 'Cause that's how I write 14.

I: I notice that when you write 14 you have a 1, and on the right of that is a 4. What does that 4 stand for?

C: 'Cause it's 14.

I: All right. What does the 1 stand for?

C: That's how you write 14.

I: Why don't you write it like this [41]?

C: That's 41.

I: All right. Why do you write 41 like that?

C: Because there's a 4 there and a 1 there.

I: Why did they invent that way of doing it? What could it possibly mean? What does that 1 stand for?

C: 1.

I: What does that 4 stand for?

C: 4.

I: Can you write the number one hundred twenty-three? That's right. That's how people write one hundred twenty-three. What does that 1 mean?

C: 1.

I: Just 1. And what does that 2 mean? What does it stand for? What is it telling us?

C: 2.

I: Just 2. And the 3? What does that tell us?

C: Just 3.

Chris has the rules necessary for the accurate writing of numbers, but can say next to nothing about the ideas behind them. His work with numbers seems entirely on an action level, and does not appear to encompass any higher levels of understanding. Chris can *operate* but not theorize.

This of course is not unusual. Children seem to approach many areas of behavioral and intellectual activity in this manner. They can ride a bicycle without being able to explain how they do it, and they can talk without being able to explain the rules of grammar. Chris is probably more typical than children who can verbalize their understanding.

In *Stage II*, children also write a number correctly without being able to explain the rationale for doing so. Yet now they imagine hypothetical alternatives that they realize are incorrect.

The interviewer asked Alice, a third grader, "How come you write 13 like that?

A: 'Cause you have to: 1 and 3.

I: Why?

A: 'Cause if you wrote it 3 and 1 it would be 31. It's the only way to do it.

So Alice realized that a hypothetical alternative would be wrong.

Another third grader, Seslie, did the following:

I: Why do you write 13 with a 1 and then to the right of the 1 a 3? Why was that 13?

S: Because if the 3 be in front of the 1 and the 1 in back of the 3 it would be 31.

I: O.K. Well why do you need two different numbers like this, a 1 followed by a 3 to make 13?

S: 'Cause if there was only 1 it would be only 1 and if there was only 3 it would be only 3. So if you had a 1 there and a 3 there you could change it any way you want to. If you put a 2 beside it, it would be 12 and a 3 beside it, it would be 13.

I: Why does it work that way?

Seslie could not answer.

Asked about 17, Sonya, a first grader said, "They put a one there so they would know it's seventeen. They could put it a different way. They could put a seven here and a one here. But they [made it 17] so they know it's seventeen instead of seventy one." Sonya saw the difference between 17 and 71, but could not say *why* the difference took the form it did. In general, Stage II children write a given number in one and one way only, and volunteer that hypothetical alternatives are wrong. At the same time, they have no explanation at all for the correct response.

In Stage III, children connect the writing of numbers with a theory of place value, and the connection appears to be genuine and meaningful.

Ronnie, a second grader, was asked, "Do you know why 13 is written like that?

R: Because it's one ten and three more.

I: Where is the ten?

R: [He pointed to 1.] Right there.

I: And where is the three more?

Ronnie pointed to the 3.

Ronnie's understanding of the place value theory of written number appears genuine because his phrasing is somewhat unique and therefore is probably not a repetition of the teacher's remarks. Thus he said, *"one ten and three more,"* rather than *"and three ones,"* which is the way the teacher probably would have said it.

Notice that Ronnie's understanding of the written numbers involves a theory that reinterprets them in terms of the decimal system. Ronnie said that 13 may be conceived of in terms of a ten and three ones. So understanding of written numbers requires the application of a theory—a view that conceptualizes the world of numbers in terms of ones, tens, hundreds, and so on. From the child's point of view, this is quite an intellectual achievement—13 could just as easily be one seven and six more (as it is in another base system).

Kathy, a second grader, also gave a very sophisticated version of place value theory.

I: Why do you write a 13 like that, a 1 followed by a 3?

K: 'Cause there's one 10, right? So you just put 1. I don't know why it's made like that. They could put 10 ones and a 3. So you see 13 is like 10 and 3, but the way we write it, it would be 103 so they just put 1 for one 10 and 3 for the extra 3 that it adds on to the 10.

In other words, Kathy knew that our system is arbitrary—"they could put 10 ones and a 3." (She did not seem to recognize, however, that this would be inefficient.) Further, she realized that 13 is an abbreviated way of writing one 10 and a 3—otherwise, it would be 103. Kathy's explanation is so spontaneous and natural that one doubts it could possibly be a parroting of a teacher's explanation.

Consider next the example of Doug, age 7.[7]

I: Why did you write a 1 followed by a 3 [to indicate 13]?

D: Because if you put a 3 followed by a 1, then it would be thirty-one. It wouldn't make sense.

I: What does 1 stand for?

D: It stands for ten, and the 3 stands for three. Ten and three is thirteen. The tens are always on the left side.

I: What if we put a 1 here and made 131? Then what does the 1 on the left stand for?

D: It stands for the hundreds.

I: So then the tens are no longer on the left.

D: No. It's between. It's like one hundred, three tens, one.

Andrea, eight years, had another kind of theory: she had written 132.

I: What does this 3 mean?

A: It's on the tens stick.

I: Tens stick? I don't see a stick there. Where do these sticks come from?

A: There's a stick in my head.

I: Where do these sticks come from?

Andrea explained that the sticks were a kind of abacus device that her teacher used in teaching arithmetic. The abacus makes obvious use of the base ten system: it has a separate place for ones, tens, and so on. Andrea then interpreted written number according to the abacus metaphor. For her, the ones place, tens place, and so on all have a literal, concrete meaning.

In brief, Stage III children do not merely write numbers correctly and know when empirical alternatives are wrong. They also interpret written numbers in terms of a theory. They see that the numbers may be conceived of as a decimal system—an arrangement in which one arbitrarily groups the world of numbers into ones, tens, hundreds, and so on. Or they think of them in terms of a concrete metaphor, like the abacus. In either event, understanding is more than writing numbers accurately or getting the right answer. Not many children reach Stage III.

SUMMARY

Young children already know a good deal of informal arithmetic when they first try to read and write mathematical symbols. Learning to write numbers is very much like learning to say them. Children have to memorize the first ten digits. But after that they learn rules, based on place value, for writing numbers above 10. Their application of these rules is at first imperfect: often they write numbers as they hear them—402 for "forty-two." But eventually they master the rules for smaller numbers and later for larger ones.

They read numbers in the same ways that they write them, and therefore may read a number like 402 as "forty-two."

Young children develop somewhat idiosyncratic interpretations of written symbols. They interpret mathematical sentences like $3 + 4 = \square$ in terms of actions. This, of course, is legitimate and stems from children's ordinary experience in school. Yet their interpretation is limited and sometimes leads to error as when children cannot understand such sentences as $3 = 3$ or $\square = 4 + 3$.

Children have some difficulty in understanding the theory of place value underlying written numbers. In Stage I, they simply write numbers correctly but have no idea of why they are written in that manner. In Stage II, they realize that other ways of writing the numbers are wrong, but still do not understand the theory. In Stage III, they relate the writing of numbers to the theory of place value. Not many children reach this stage.

PRINCIPLES

1. *Children's understanding of written symbolism generally lags behind their informal arithmetic.* Paul could count to a million but only write the symbol 1. While children can often add decently enough, they cannot read or write $2 + 1 = 3$. In general, children's informal arithmetic is powerful, their understanding of written symbolism weak.

2. *Children interpret written symbolism in terms of what they already know.* They write numbers as they have already learned to say them. They read mathematical sentences in terms of the computational actions they already know how to perform. In Piaget's terms, children *assimilate* the written system into their previously existing schemes. Sometimes such assimilation leads to errors, as when children believe that "thirty-three" must be written as 303. Sometimes, however, it leads to a sound understanding, as when children think of place value in terms of an abacus.

COMPUTING: THE CHILD'S SECRET INVENTIONS

A good deal of elementary school education is devoted to addition, subtraction, multiplication, and division with whole numbers. Children first add and subtract with small numbers and then they repeat the operations with larger ones and then larger still. They are taught standard methods of computation. These *algorithms,* developed and codified over the course of centuries, are guaranteed to achieve the correct result; applied properly, they always work. So formal education tries to make available to children some powerful procedures. But what use do children make of their cultural legacy? We shall see that they often ignore the standard procedures and instead rely on methods of their own invention.

Algorithms

In the early school years, children devote considerable effort to learning the number facts—$2 + 2 = 4$, and so on—and the standard methods of computation based on them. Children learn that given

$$\begin{array}{r} 24 \\ + 35 \end{array}$$,you add downward from the right. You have to remember

$4 + 5$ first, write that down, and then add $2 + 3$, writing that down. This algorithm is based on the place value system: you can add the 4 and 5 because in our system they represent ones; and you can add the 2 and 3 because they stand for tens. You break up 24 and 35 into $(20 + 4)$ and $(30 + 5)$. Then you add the 4 and 5 and the 20 and 30.

What is there to say about children's learning and understanding algorithms like these? Anyone who has been to school knows some very simple truths about the learning of algorithms: some children learn to do algorithms properly but do not really understand them. We do not need detailed psychological proofs of facts as obvious as these. What is interesting is the rare case of a child who *does* understand the algorithms.

Doug, who as we have seen displayed a sound appreciation of place value theory, was asked to add $13 + 36$. He got the correct answer, 49. How? "Add 10 to 30 and you get 40 and then you add 6 and 3 which makes 9, so 49." He explained further: "the one [in 13] stands for 10; and then you see the 3 over here in [in 36] stands for 30 which is three tens, then four tens, like they hook up to each other and make four." He meant that if you add the 1 in 13 and the 3 in 36, the result is four tens or 40. "And then these two [the 3 in 13 and the 6 in 36] are hooked up to make 9. It's like they're both hooked up and then they both hook up to each other and make 49."

In brief, Doug appreciated the place value approach to writing numbers and seemed to understand that column addition proceeds by "hooking up" numbers of like value.

No doubt Doug's understanding was quite unusual for a seven-year-old. The more typical case is that of the child who learns to compute in the standard manner, perhaps with some inaccuracy, but understands little of what he does.

Invented procedures

Sometimes we think or like to believe that children do as they are taught. But this is not always true, and it is certainly not true so far as computation is concerned. Despite all the effort expended in teaching algorithms, children often do not use them. Instead of exploiting the very real power of these standard procedures, children often use other methods entirely. They assimilate school mathematics into their own mental framework: the result is *invented procedures*, methods that are partly based on codified written arithmetic, and partly on the child's distinctive approach. Often children find their invented methods more comfortable than the algorithms taught in school.

Counting methods

Suppose children are given a written problem, like $2 + 3 = ?$ or an oral one, like "two plus three is . . .?" They do not need to decide whether to add or subtract. They know addition should be performed; they just have to do it. The question is *how*.

Children often use counting methods to solve simple addition or subtraction problems. At 7–3, Rebecca was given $5 + \square = 9$.

I: Five and what makes nine?

R: Four.

I: How did you know that?

R: 'Cause, five and then six, seven, eight, nine. [She counted on her fingers.]

She used the same strategy for analogous subtraction problems like $5 - 3 = \square$.

Counting methods seem to be extremely common.[8] In the first grade, almost all children who manage to succeed on elementary

---

Sonya's Words of Wisdom

A first grader, Sonya, had some important things to say about computation.

I: How would you do five and five?

S: I'd count, you know. But it's noisy in this room, so while I was counting I'd think, I'd concentrate.

*   *   *

I: You were a little confused when you said eight and four is eleven.

S: Yes, because once my brother and I, we were playing something. We were doing a work sheet. My brother had eight and four and he put eleven. He put down eleven and it got me all confused.

*   *   *

S: Some people say six plus three is eight. They get their answers wrong.

*   *   *

I: What are you doing in math?

S: Well, it gives me a lot to think about. I know how to do two and two. I just gotta learn how to do math.

---

addition problems (like $4 + 3$, or $7 + 12$, or $23 + 13$) do so by employing some kind of counting method. They count on their fingers, they count tallies, they count starting at one, or they count on from the larger number. They seldom use even so simple a method as remembering the number facts. By the time they reach the second grade, only about half the children who succeed do so by counting. The half who do count use the efficient procedure of counting on from the larger number. This is the method we saw Rebecca using earlier: to add $5 + 3$, you do 5, 6, 7, 8. It is obviously less work than adding $5 + 3$ by counting from the beginning: 1, 2, 3, . . . 8. In brief, as children get more experience in counting, their methods become more efficient.

The tendency to use counting in addition seems to persist even into the later grades (and no doubt into adulthood). Seventh grade children do essentially the same thing that Rebecca and Houlihan's students did. "For example, when a pupil was thinking of 9 + 8 = ? he said '10, 11, 12, 13, 14, 15, 16, 17.' He was likely to have means to tell him when to stop counting. Most pupils use their fingers for this purpose."[9]

So children often use counting methods to do addition, subtraction, and multiplication. Indeed, I have seen children use such methods even when the numbers are relatively large, as in 83 + 19. No doubt the proportion of children using counting at each grade level varies to some extent according to the nature of the curriculum. If counting were permitted or emphasized in class, probably more children would use it than if it were discouraged. While the proportions may vary, the remarkable fact is that many young children do not add or subtract by remembering number facts or by using standing algorithms; they calculate by means of invented counting methods, often involving use of the fingers.

How do we know that these counting methods are invented? There are several kinds of evidence. One is that preschoolers and children who do not go to school also use counting methods to do practical arithmetic. As I showed in Chapter 3, counting methods exist all over the world, in many cultures, in schooled and unschooled children. Counting is the natural method for doing arithmetic. We should therefore not be surprised if children continue to use it when they get to school. A second proof is that we have seen counting methods used in classes where the teacher actively discourages them. Often when we interview children we observe them counting surreptitiously on their fingers under the table; when asked, they say the teacher has told them that counting in this manner is forbidden and they expect a reprimand. A third proof is related to the second. Some children who fail miserably in school and whose teachers think they are capable of virtually nothing can nevertheless calculate quite well by means of counting methods. The teachers are quite surprised by this competence; surely they did not teach it.

So it seems fair to say that children's counting methods are invented. They apply the counting procedures they already know and use in connection with real objects to the arithmetic problems encountered in school. Invented procedures are often more comfortable than those taught in school.

Counting mixed with algorithms

With experience, children improve their invented counting methods. They eliminate some of the drudgery of counting by exploiting some remembered number facts and algorithms.

Danny, 7–6, was asked how much is 7 and 7.

D: 14.

I: And how did you get it?

D: I said, 6 and 6 are 12. Put 2 more there makes 14.

In this case, Danny could not use the easiest method—namely remembering that 7 and 7 are 14—to solve the problem. Consequently, he had to devise an alternative approach. His solution was to transform the original problem into one he could deal with. This involved several steps. First, he took away one from each of the sevens. Second, this left him with 6 + 6, the sum of which he did remember. Third, he counted on the ones, which he had earlier taken from the sevens, and thus got the correct sum of 14.

Danny frequently used invented methods of the type described above. For example, later on in the interview he was asked to find the sum of 12 and 6.

D: 18. Because 10 plus 6 are 16. Add 2 more to it and it is 18.

Later the interviewer asked Danny, "What plus 9 will give you 12?"

D: 2 . . . 2 . . . 3!

I: 3, why would you say 3?

D: Because 10 and 2 is 12 and take 1 away from the 10 and add that one to the 2.

So Danny *rearranged* problems in such a way as to exploit the number facts he remembered; after that, whatever needed to be done could be accomplished by counting.

Throughout elementary school and no doubt beyond, memory for number facts combined with counting is used as a basis for the solution of various arithmetic problems, not just addition. Lankford reports that, of a total of 176 seventh grade pupils whom he interviewed, "surprisingly there were 63 pupils who used counting in the multiplication of whole numbers."[10] Often (thirty-one cases) counting was used when the child was deriving an unknown combination from a known one. For example, a pupil who did not know the combination $7 \times 8 = ?$ said, "$7 \times 7 = 49$, 50, 51, 52, 53, 54, 55, 56." He stopped when he had counted seven fingers after the 49.

Kathy, a second grader, offers a graphic example of multiplication by counting and other more formal procedures. She was shown a paper with six dots on it.

> I: Suppose I have twelve identical pieces of paper like this . . . Can you tell me how you would find out how many dots you had altogether?
>
> K: I'd probably count them like this, 'cause you know it's too hard to count by sixes.
>
> I: How are you going to find out how many dots we have altogether? There are 12 sheets. We have six dots on a sheet.
>
> K: I'd probably count them up on my fingers. 1, 2, 3 . . . 16, 17, 18.

She pointed to each dot as she counted. But she neglected to keep track of how many times she had counted the group of six.

> K: How many is that?
>
> I: I don't know. Somehow you have got to keep track, don't you?
>
> K: O.K. Here goes. 1, 2, 3 . . .

She pointed to each dot with her left hand as she counted. Then, after she counted each group of six, she held up one finger of her right hand. In this way she kept track of the number of groups of six. She counted the group of six five times, getting 30.

> K: So now I've counted it five times. Let's see, 30 another time, that would be 60 counted ten times.
>
> I: How many times do you want to count it altogether?
>
> K: 12. Let's see. 61, 62, 63 . . . 71, 72 . . . 72 dots.

In brief, after Kathy counted to reach $5 \times 6 = 30$, she doubled the 30, realizing that this would give 10×6. Next, she counted on by ones again to reach the total of 72. Kathy thus used a combination of counting and doubling to solve the multiplication problem.

Carol, age eight, probably gets the prize for the number of different techniques used in an invented procedure. The interviewer began by establishing that Carol knew that there were seven days in a week, and twenty-four hours in a day. Then he asked, "How many hours in a week?" and "What do you do to get the answer?" Carol did not conceptualize the problem in terms of multiplication. She replied, "just add them up," and wrote the following column of numbers:

$$
\begin{array}{r}
24 \\
24 \\
24 \\
24 \\
24 \\
24 \\
\underline{24} \\
\end{array}
$$

Then she used a combination of procedures to solve the problem. She began by adding the first four fours in the column.

C: 4 and 4 is 8. 8 and 8 is 16.

Note that Carol added the first two fours to get 8; implicitly added the second two fours to get 8; and then added the first two sums to get 16.
Then she continued.

C: 16, 17, 18, 19, 20, 21, 22, 23, 24, 25, 26, 27, 28. That's 28.

So after adding 8 and 8 to get 16, Carol used a counting procedure to reach 28. Next she employed a different method.

C: I put 8 down and then I carried the 2 up there. I brought it upstairs.

She wrote:

$$
\begin{array}{r}
^{2}24 \\
24 \\
24 \\
24 \\
24 \\
24 \\
\underline{24} \\
8 \\
\end{array}
$$

C: Then all I have to do is . . . 8 × 2 . . . [she wrote down 16] . . . 168.

So Carol finished the problem by multiplying.

Instead of employing the conventional method of solution that she had been taught, Carol assimilated the problem into her own framework. She used a rather unique strategy, involving a variety of computational methods; first she regrouped and added, then she counted, then she carried, and finally she multiplied. All this to find the sum of a column of numbers!

How does the use of invented strategies develop with age? While first graders' invented strategies consist almost exclusively of counting, second graders' often involve a mixture of remembered number facts and counting. Indeed these invented methods can be quite effective. Those second graders who use them seem to do better at school arithmetic than children who do not.[11]

Using simpler methods for harder ones

One side of children's nature is *conservative*. They continually draw on what they already know to solve new problems. They rely on familiar techniques as long as possible before learning new methods. And then, when learning is necessary, they mould the new as thoroughly as they can to fit the old. In Piaget's terms, this is *assimilation*, "the prime fact of mental life."

We have already seen assimilation at work in children's use of counting for addition; in their idiosyncratic combination of remembered number facts with counting; and in their invention of combinations of methods. Now we will see how they assimilate the harder operations, like subtraction and multiplication, into simpler schemes like addition.

Ralph, an eight-year-old, was asked to do "7 take away 3." He got the right answer. How? "Since 4 plus 3 is 7, 7 take away 3 is 4." Ralph knew that subtraction is just the reverse of addition and therefore used a remembered fact from addition to solve a subtraction problem.

Lori, in the third grade, was asked, "How much less is 382 than 400?" She also solved the problem by converting to addition, in three steps. First she wrote:

$$382$$
$$+ \underline{}$$

then

$$382$$
$$+ \, 28$$
$$\overline{0}$$

then

$$382$$
$$+ \, 18$$
$$\overline{400}$$

Subtraction was too hard for Lori to use with numbers of this magnitude, so she used addition, a more comfortable, although cumbersome, procedure.

Children often convert multiplication into addition. Chris, twelve years old, was shown a 6 × 8 rectangular array of boxes and asked to figure out the total number of boxes in the array. Chris said that he would do "6 times 8."

I: 6 × 8. Okay why don't you write that down?

C: 6 × 8 is . . . [Chris wrote down 6 + 6 + 6 + 6 + 6 + 6 + 6 + 6].

I: O.K. Do you expect to get the same answer from this problem [referring to the 6 + 6, etc.] as this problem [referring to the 6 × 8]?

C: 48.

I: O.K. How did you get 48?

C: Well I did four sixes . . . I mean I added them together. And then I added; the answer was 24. Like 24, so I added them together, and that was 48. [Chris wrote down 24 + 24 = 48.]

In other words, when Chris attempted to do 6 × 8, he converted the problem into addition, writing down 6 + 6, etc. He then solved the addition problem by breaking it into two smaller problems, namely 6 + 6 + 6 + 6 = 24 and 6 + 6 + 6 + 6 = 24, and adding the two 24's. Chris's solution relied on some elementary facts and procedures that he already knew.

Similarly, Peter, a thirteen-year-old, was given the following problem:

I: Suppose you have 48 divided by 6. Go ahead. Do it any way you want.

P: [He wrote a 7 in the quotient's place.] Wait . . . 8.

I: How do you know that's right?

P: Cause 6 × 6 is 36 and add 7 more to it and that's going to make 42 and another 8 more would be 48.

Peter's strategy seems to have been the following. First, he converted the division problem (48 divided by 6) into one involving multiplication (6 × ? = 48). But he could not remember that 6 × 8 = 48, which would have given him the answer. Consequently, he had to use a combination of methods. He began by drawing on what he already knew, namely that 6 × 6 = 36. Then he acknowledged an equivalence between multiplication and repeated addition. He added 6 to 36, which told him how much is 6 × 7. As he described this, he mistakenly *said*, "Add 7 to 36." But this seemed to *mean*: if you add 6 to 36 you get the same result as when you multiply 6 × 7. Then Peter added 6 to 42, which told him how much is 6 × 8 and gave him the missing multiplier, 8. Again he described his computations incorrectly ("another 8 more would be 48"); but, again, verbal mistakes only obscure his understanding of the relation between multiplication and addition.

So Peter transformed a division problem to multiplication; used a multiplication fact he remembered; and went on to use addition to solve a multiplication problem. At the same time, he could not accurately describe what he was doing!

On another occasion, Peter assimilated multiplication into addition. In the course of a division problem, Peter had to determine what number times 23 would yield a product less than 198. He began by multiplying 11 × 23 and then 10 × 23, and in both cases got a product larger than 198. After seeing that 11 and 10 did not work, he tried this apparently strange computation:

$$
\begin{array}{r}
23 \\
\times\ 5 \\
\hline
115 \\
23 \\
\hline
148
\end{array}
$$

I: What did you do there? You got 115, right?

P: And I added 23 more to it, and it came out 148.

He had made a simple calculational error (he should have gotten 138). But what was the point of the addition?

I: Why did you add 23?

P: To see how close I could get if I added another 23.

I: Why did you add? You were multiplying before.

P: Then I added 23 and it came out 148.

I: What is another way of getting 148?

P: By adding 23 × 6.

What was happening in this sequence? Peter first found that 5 × 23 is 115. Then he added 23 to the 115 (and got an incorrect answer, 148). He did this addition because he realized that it was an alternative method of finding 6 × 23. In other words, he saw the equivalence between multiplication and repeated addition. This perception was most likely at an implicit level. Peter did not have the formal knowledge to say, "multiplication is repeated addition." Nevertheless, his calculational performance was governed by this rule.

This sophistication stands in marked contrast to some other features of Peter's behavior: he made an elementary error of calculation (115 + 23 = 148) and he could not talk very well about multiplication (he said, "by *adding* 23 × 6").

The previous example was no fluke. Peter went on to do:

$$
\begin{array}{r}
23 \\
\times\ 5 \\
\hline
115 \\
23 \\
\hline
148 \\
23 \\
\hline
171 \\
23 \\
\hline
184
\end{array}
$$

He was continuing his repeated addition (with a fortuitous calculational error that corrected his previous error). Moreover, when he got the sum 148, he said, "six"; when he got 171, he said "seven"; and when he got 184, he said, "eight." This seems to indicate very clearly that he was identifying the sums as the equivalents of 6 × 23, 7 × 23, and 8 × 23. In short, Peter clearly assimilated multiplication into addition.

Children convert fractions into addition too. The interviewer showed Jane, at 9–6, thirty small blocks.

I: How many are half of these?

J: 15.

I: Can you prove that? Can you convince me it's true?

J: I don't think so.

I: O.K. How many is a quarter of these blocks? One fourth?

Jane was silent. She looked puzzled.

I: That might be too tough. I won't ask you that.

J: Wait . . . 5 and ½ . . . 7 and ½.

I: Very good. Now tell me how you got 7 and ½.

J: I did 8 and 8 is 16, and so that's just one more, so it would be 7½.

Jane's strategy, despite her inability to express it fully, is nevertheless clear. She knew already that 15 is one half of 30, probably since 15 + 15 = 30. Then to find ¼ of 30, she attempted to find that number which when added to itself would give 15. In other words, she knew on an implicit, action level that ¼ + ¼ = ½. But to get half of 15, it would be necessary to take a roundabout route. She tried 8, and found that 8 + 8 = 16; unfortunately, 16 was one more than she needed. She got rid of the extra one by subtracting half of it from each 8, thus obtaining the correct answer, 7½. Jane's strategy is quite sensible, if awkward.

Novelties

If one aspect of children's nature is conservative, the other is innovative. Again in Piaget's terms, children not only assimilate, they *accommodate*. They respond to environmental challenges by developing new methods of solution. In addition to relying on what is familiar, they develop novel approaches.* In arithmetic, the novel approaches take several forms, ranging from the rearrangement of terms to the invention of new algorithms.

At six years, Roberta was given a rather colorful problem involv-

---

*According to Piaget, every act contains elements of both assimilation and accommodation, the old and the new. Thus, while Jane's method for doing fractions relied on what she already knew, like "eight and eight is sixteen," it also contained novel elements, like the subtraction of half the one from each 8. As is well known, Piaget's thought is quite complex and difficult to understand. For an introduction, see Ginsburg, H. and Opper, S. *Piaget's theory of intellectual development: an introduction* (Englewood Cliffs, N.J.: Prentice-Hall, 1969).

ing a monster who had four heads and sixty-four hairs on each head.[12] How many hairs did the monster have altogether? Roberta said, "Sixty-four . . . a hundred and twenty . . . two hundred and forty . . . and sixteen added onto two hundred and forty is two hundred and fifty-six."

Instead of doing 4×64, Roberta converted it into an addition problem (this aspect is conservative). But adding $64 + 64 + 64 + 64$ was too hard. Therefore, she converted the problem into $(60 + 60 + 60 + 60) + (4 + 4 + 4 + 4)$ (that was the innovative part). She did this first solving for $60 + 60$, getting 120, and then doubling that to get 240. Next she added on the 16.

This is a very sensible procedure: it is often easier to calculate with the numbers rearranged than otherwise. Indeed, Roberta's procedure took into account the notion of place value: she added tens separately and units separately.

Another example involves Lori, a third grader, who was asked to add 83 and 5 and 294. She did it in her head: "Well 294, is almost in the three hundreds. Then 5 more is 299 . . . What's the other number?" The interviewer told her. She then said, "It'd be 382." To do this she rearranged the order of the numbers in the problem as originally presented to her. She first added 294 and 5, which is easy to do mentally. This yields a sum, 299, which also happens to be easy to add mentally to the subsequent two-digit number: simply take away one from the 83. In brief, by a clever rearrangement of the order of numbers, Lori took advantage of certain properties that allowed her to do easy mental calculation.

Kathy, in the second grade, also rearranged the numbers in an addition problem. Asked to add 123 and 52 and 4, she wrote down the numbers as follows:

```
52                    123
 4
```

First she examined the tens column of the 52 and the 123. She counted on from 20, five times, by tens to reach 70. She said, "it never changes," meaning the 1 in the hundreds column. She then wrote:

```
52                    123
 4                      1
                        1
```

"So I just put 1, 1, 1. But then I add the number [5]." She wrote:

52	123
4	173
	1

Then she added the 4 to 173 and got 177 writing:

52	123
4	173
	177

Next she noticed that she had forgotten to add in the 2 from 52. She added it on to get 179.

Kathy's invented method involved adding numbers in a convenient sequence and in a manner that takes account of place value theory. Of course, the standard addition algorithm does essentially the same thing. But like Roberta, Kathy preferred her own sequence of operations.

Peter used an interesting principle to rearrange numbers for division.

I: This time we won't write all this out, we'll use some guessing. Suppose I have 10 and make that go into 150. Can you guess how much that would be without having to figure it out?

P: Yes, 2 . . . 15.

I: Write that down. Sure of that?

P: Yes.

I: What do you mean?

P: Because there are five 10's in 50, and five more in 100, and another 15 in 150.

Later Peter's language was clearer. Given 10 into 1,500, he answered, 150. Why? "Because there's 100 10's in 1,000, and 50 10's in 500, so they make 150 altogether." Peter transformed the problem from 1,500 divided by 10 into 500 divided by 10, plus 500 divided by 10, plus 500 divided by 10. This then becomes 50 + 50 + 50 = 150. In other words, he was using the distributive law for division, although no doubt he could not state it explicitly. In any event, he transformed one division problem, usually solved by standard calculations, into another division problem that could be solved mentally.

Some children develop genuinely interesting invented procedures, and one of the most remarkable of these is that developed by Kye, an eight-year-old.[13] Kye's teacher had written on the board:

$$64$$
$$- 28$$

and she was explaining that "you can't take 8 from 4, so you have to regroup the 64 as . . . "

At this point, Kye interrupted.

Kye said, "Oh, yes you can. 4 minus 8 is negative 4." He wrote:

$$64$$
$$- 28$$
$$- 4$$

"And 40 and negative 4 give you 36 . . . the answer is 36." He wrote:

$$64$$
$$- 28$$
$$- 4$$
$$40$$
$$36$$

In brief, Kye subtracted 8 from 4, getting negative 4; he subtracted 20 from 60 getting 40; and then he added negative 4 to the 40, getting 36, which is the correct answer.

The writers comment: "This surely deserves to be described as one of the nicest algorithms for subtracting that we have ever seen . . . and it is the *bona fide* creation (or, if you prefer, 'discovery') of a third grade boy in Weston, Connecticut. Prior to Kye's showing us his method, it was not known to any teacher or mathematician of our acquaintance."

SUMMARY

Sometimes children solve arithmetic problems by means of the standard methods—algorithms—taught in school. Applied properly, these always work and are superior to children's informal methods.

But often children do not use the algorithms as taught. Instead they use invented procedures of several types. Sometimes they solve arithmetic problems by counting methods of one kind or another, like addition by counting on from the larger number. Sometimes they combine counting methods with remembered addition facts and algorithms. Thus, to add they use whatever addition facts they remember and count on from there. Sometimes they convert difficult problems into simpler ones, as when they solve a multiplication problem by adding. And occasionally they develop novel approaches, as when they use clever regrouping strategies to facilitate addition.

PRINCIPLES

1. *Children do not always do arithmetic as taught.* To be sure, children sometimes use standard methods to compute, especially when the teacher tells them what to do. But often they use their own, at least partially invented procedures. This is yet another example of *assimilation.* Children are not a blank slate when they learn school arithmetic. They already possess practical techniques for adding and subtracting; they already have their own ideas about mathematics. They then transform what they are taught in accordance with what they know, and the result is invented procedures for arithmetic.

2. *Children's invented methods rely heavily on counting.* Just as counting forms the basis for preschool children's practical arithmetic, so is counting essential for schoolchildren's invented procedures. Especially when all else fails, children add, subtract, and multiply by counting. With counting as a secure underpinning, they can go on to develop invented strategies of some subtlety. Also, counting is firm, comfortable knowledge that can be used to assimilate difficult, strange algorithms.

Chapter 6

Mistakes

Children often make mistakes in school arithmetic. They fail to master the standard computational techniques and produce wrong answers. School failure is obvious, but its causes remain obscure. Why do children make errors, and what can be done to help children eliminate them? In an attempt to answer these questions, we first examine the nature and causes of children's errors. It is not helpful to explain mistakes in terms of low intelligence or low mathematical aptitude. Concepts like these obscure the fact that errors result from systematic strategies that often have sensible origins. Like their accurate answers, children's errors are often produced by idiosyncratic but meaningful strategies. Second, we examine the real-life pattern of errors and successes. Children can be extraordinarily inconsistent: at the same time as they use distorted strategies to get wrong answers, they use powerful computations to get right ones. This fact suggests some approaches to helping children with problems. Third, we examine gaps between hidden competencies and school performance. We shall see that in almost every case children failing in school nevertheless possess hidden competencies of an informal nature. Nourishment of these normally ignored strengths is the most important single key to effective teaching.

THE NATURE AND ORIGINS OF MISTAKES

A child adds $52 + 123 + 4$ and gets 17. Another subtracts $15 - 7$ and gets 65. These are blatant errors, absurd mistakes. If you saw them as answers to a test, what would you conclude? One possibility is that the child does not know either how to add or subtract and was just guessing. Another possibility is that the child suffers from deficient intelligence: he has a low IQ, perhaps as a result of cultural deprivation, and hence cannot master the techniques of arithmetic. A third possibility is that the child possesses low mathematical aptitude or perhaps a learning disability, either of which could prevent him from doing accurate arithmetic.

I believe that these explanations are unhelpful: incorrect answers are seldom due to guessing, to low intelligence, or to low mathematical aptitude. Explanations like these, while occasionally useful, most often serve to mask ignorance of how children really go about doing their school arithmetic. If these explanations are misguided, what is the main cause of children's errors? A close look shows that they derive from systematic procedures having sensible origins.

Mistakes are based on rules

Sherry, a third grader, was the child asked to add 52 + 123 + 4. She got 17, an apparently absurd answer—so absurd that it must have been the result of an unthinking guess. Was it? The interviewer asked, "How did you get it?" Sherry replied; "First I added 5 and 2 and then I added 1 and 4 and the 2 and 3." In other words, Sherry simply added the individual digits without regard to place value.

Theresa, a second grader, was asked to add:

$$24$$
$$+\ 53$$

She gave the answer 68. Was it a guess? No, there was a specific rationale for the answer. Theresa added *sideways* to get the result. She added the 2 and 4 in 24 to get the 6, and the 5 and 3 in 53 to get the 8. Again, a systematic, organized procedure.

In doing subtraction, many children use the following misguided but systematic procedure. Asked to do:

$$21$$
$$-\ 5$$

Bob came up with the answer 24. He had subtracted 1 from 5 to get 4 and then simply brought down the 2 (or subtracted 0 from it).[1]

Ralph used a similar technique. Asked to subtract seven cents from fifteen cents, he wrote down:

$$15¢$$
$$-\ 7¢$$
$$65¢$$

He lined up the numbers incorrectly from left to right and then subtracted the 1 from the 7 and brought down the 5 to get 65.[2]

Neither Bob nor Ralph used borrowing, which could have
yielded the right answer. Instead, both used the common misguided
technique of *always subtract the smaller number from the larger.*

Like Ralph, many children have especial difficulty in lining up
numbers properly. Joe, eleven years of age, in grade five, was given a
problem in which the numbers were deliberately arranged in an
improper allignment:

$$\begin{array}{r} 14 \\ 37 \\ 7 \\ \hline 3,406 \end{array}$$

His response was simply to add downward, using the alignment
given. Was Joe simply trying to humor the interviewer by doing the
problem as presented? No. His difficulties with alignment persisted
in the absence of adult suggestion. Later he was asked to write down
some numbers for addition. The interviewer said, "Nineteen, four
hundred seventy two, three. . . ." Joe wrote:

$$\begin{array}{r} 19 \\ 472 \\ 3 \\ \hline \end{array}$$

and proceeded to add downward as before.

Joe's mistakes in addition were not capricious. When he lined
up the numbers he used the rule, *line up numbers on the left and
add downward.* When the numbers were already aligned (properly
or not), he used the rule *add downward.* Children often use several
different faulty procedures, each resulting in a different kind of error.

Benny, a twelve-year-old, used an interesting but faulty rule for
converting fractions to decimals. It may be illustrated as follows:

I: How would you write two tenths as a decimal or decimal fraction?

B: 1 point 2. [Benny wrote 1.2]

I: And 5 over 10?

B: 1 point 5.

Benny was able to describe his incorrect procedure. For

example, in explaining how 5/10 equals 1.5, Benny said, "The 1 stands for 10, the decimal; then there's 5 . . . shows how many 1's." In another example Benny wrote 400/400 equals 8.00 because "the numbers are the same . . . say like 4,000 over 5,000. [Benny is referring to the number of digits in each case.] All you do is add them up; put the answer down; then put your decimal in the right place . . . in front of the [last] three numbers."

This incorrect procedure allowed Benny to convert any fraction to a decimal. For example, 429/100 equals 5.29, 3/1000 equals 1.003, and 27/15 equals 4.2. The following example makes the matter extremely clear.

I: And 4 over 11?

B: 1 point 5.

I: Now does it matter if we change this [4/11] and say that it is 11/4?

B: It won't change at all; it will be the same thing . . . 1 point 5.

Benny used the same procedure in the reverse direction.

I: How would you write point 5 as an ordinary fraction?

B: Point 5 . . . It would be like this . . . 3 over 2 or 2 over 3 or anything as long as it comes out with the answer 5 because you are adding them.[3]

We see then that Benny's behavior was both bizarre and perfectly logical. The answers he came up with were unique: no doubt very few children make similar errors. At the same time, his behavior was organized and regular; he followed his (strange) rules very consistently.

The origins of incorrect rules

We have seen that children make mistakes because they use faulty rules. The next and obvious question is this: where do these rules come from? Surely they are not taught as such. Do children just invent them on their own? No. The answer seems to be that the faulty rules have sensible origins. Children's mistaken procedures are in fact good rules badly applied or distorted to some degree.

Here is an example involving Chris, a twelve-year-old, who was asked to set himself a simple multiplication problem. Chris wrote the following problem and solution:

$$\begin{array}{r} {}^{1}20 \\ \times\ 6 \\ \hline 0 \\ 32 \\ \hline 32 \end{array}$$

The interview revealed that Chris's reasoning was essentially this: 6 times 0 is 0 and you write that down. And 6 times 2 is 12. Write down the 2 below the 0. Carry the 1 and add it to the 2. This gives the 3 in 32. Add 32 to 0 to get 32 as the answer.

Chris's mistake was again based on a systematic, but incorrect procedure, a combination of multiplication and addition. How did he develop such a procedure? Certainly he did not invent it on some kind of random basis. Apparently, when Chris was faced with the new task of learning the standard multiplication algorithm, he tried to assimilate it to addition, which was already familiar. He therefore interpreted the operations of multiplication in terms of those for addition. This resulted in a unique and distorted strategy—an addition-multiplication hybrid. Chris's method is surely wrong, but it is systematic and it originates in what he already knows.

Other children (like Erlwanger's Benny) interpret operations on fractions in terms of the addition of whole numbers. One child did $\frac{3}{4} + \frac{5}{2} = 86$ because "5 + 3 = 8 and 4 + 2 = 6." Another child did $\frac{3}{4} + \frac{5}{2} = 59$, since "4 + 5 is 9; 3 + 2 is 5." Still another said that $\frac{3}{8} + \frac{7}{8} = 26$, since "7 over 8 is 15; 3 over 8 is 11; 15 + 11 = 26."[4] Again mistakes were obviously the result of an incorrect but systematic procedure. Further, the incorrect procedure had its roots in a sensible one. The children assimilated the addition of fractions into the addition of whole numbers. They misapplied a sensible method.

Bob's case shows why the child might consider some inaccurate methods to be quite reasonable.[5] A fifth grader, he was asked to add 158 + 265 + 98 and began by adding 8 + 5 + 8 to get 21. He wrote:

$$\begin{array}{r} 1\overset{1}{5}8 \\ 265 \\ 98 \\ \hline 2 \end{array}$$

He said, "I take the 2 and write it down here [in the units column] and carry the 1." The interviewer asked him why he did that. He replied, "I carried, so I put the big number down here."

Bob's rule was very simple. Instead of carrying the tens digit, whatever its value, he always carried the smaller of the two numbers obtained by adding the units column. Thus, given 23 + 9 + 9, he would do:

$$
\begin{array}{r}
^{1}23 \\
9 \\
+\ 9 \\
\hline
32
\end{array}
$$

and given 23 + 9 he would do:

$$
\begin{array}{r}
23 \\
+\ 9 \\
\hline
32
\end{array}
$$

and get exactly the same answer in both cases!

How could such a rule have originated? Bob's earliest carrying problems no doubt involved two number cases like 23 + 19 or 36 + 17. In almost all these cases, it so happens that you can carry by placing in the units column the larger of the two numbers and carrying the smallest.* Thus:

$$
\begin{array}{r}
^{1}23 \\
19 \\
\hline
42
\end{array}
\qquad
\begin{array}{r}
^{1}36 \\
17 \\
\hline
53
\end{array}
\qquad
\begin{array}{r}
^{1}79 \\
19 \\
\hline
98
\end{array}
$$

We see then that Bob's rule was a response to what he saw in his first carrying problems. The rule originated in his experience, and his invention of the rule was in a sense a creative act. Of course, it was a misguided creative act. Bob had experienced a special and unusual case and from that developed a rule that could not apply to all problems of addition. Bob overgeneralized. Yet this should not obscure the fact that his rule was based on sound observation: it had sensible origins.

*This is so because in two number problems the largest units sum has to be 18 and the smallest 10. The only exceptions to the rule are when 5 + 5 or 5 + 6 are involved in the units column.

It is not hard to see how the child can develop faulty rules of the type we have reviewed. The child's textbooks and instruction are often lacking in several ways. Mathematical principles are explained badly; little attention is given to the individual child's questions. If the material is presented badly, is it any wonder that the child creates distorted rules?

Arithmetic as an arbitrary game

Suppose that children often make mistakes. What do they think of arithmetic? Do they know that they have erred, or that there are right and wrong answers? Not necessarily. Some children believe that arithmetic is arbitrary: hence, there can be no mistakes. Thus, Seslie, a third grader, was asked to add 123 + 52 + 4. She wrote the numbers down, misaligning them:

$$
\begin{array}{r}
123 \\
52 \\
\underline{4} \\
219
\end{array}
$$

She got 219 by doing 3 + 2 + 4 = 9; then 12 (from the 123) + 5 + 4 = 21. Then 21 combined with 9 is 219.

The interviewer attempted to correct her. He did the problem properly.

S: You did it different. I put the 4 in the middle.

I: Why did I put the 4 all the way over there?

S: Probably because you wanted to. You wanted to add this together [3, 2, 4] and this [2, 5] and this [1] go over here.

Seslie seemed to think that the interviewer's procedure was arbitrary—that one can do addition any way one wants to. He asked her to do the problem again. This time she did it properly, adding 3 + 2 + 4 to get 9 and then 12 + 5 to get 17, with the overall answer 179.

But which answer did she think was correct? 219! She had no good reason for this. She just *preferred* it. For Seslie, one calculational method is about as good (non-sensical?) as another. To decide among them seems a matter of caprice.

Kathy, a second grader, was given the same problem. Once she did it correctly, getting 179 as the answer. Later she was asked to do the problem again and the interviewer lined it up improperly.

$$\begin{array}{r} 123 \\ 52 \\ \underline{4} \end{array}$$

She added downward and got 683.

I: Is that right?

K: Don't ask me. I was gonna ask you that question. Well, if you do it this way it's a different number and if you do it another way it's a different number.

I: What went wrong, if anything?

K: You put this over here [meaning the 52 in the wrong column].

I: Is there anything wrong with putting it over there?

K: No, there's nothing wrong; it just makes the number more.

I: Is your answer [683] right though?

She nodded yes. Like Seslie, Kathy seemed to believe that addition is arbitrary and hence failed to see her answer as a mistake.

Mat, an eleven-year-old in the fifth grade, felt that there are many games involved in school mathematics. There was an individualized instruction [I.I.] math made up by the "I.I. people," and another program, Urbana math, which was developed by the computers at the University of Illinois. He felt that you learn mathematics because "it's a subject of school . . . probably half the things you learn at school are not used outside." Given a problem, you try out one method. If that does not work, "the teacher would tell me what method they wanted . . . you get a different answer every method you use." The interviewer asked how Mat decided which answer is right. He replied, "It depends on which method you are told to use . . . you use that method and you come out with the answer. And that's the answer in the answer book, so that's what answer they use."[6]

The child can even justify his wrong answers in clever ways. George, a nine-year-old third grader, subtracted as follows:

$$\begin{array}{r} 14 \\ -\ 5 \\ \hline 11 \end{array}$$

He had followed the common rule of subtracting the smaller from the larger.[7] The interviewer then asked him to solve the problem by means of paper clips. The interviewer's reasoning was that he would start with fourteen clips, take away five, and see that he had nine left. But, instead, George counted out five clips and subtracted four to get one. Then he put out another one clip. In this way did he justify $14 - 5 = 11$.

Later George did another problem incorrectly and justified his answer in the same way. Shown the correct way to solve the problem, he maintained that *both* methods were correct. The interviewer's method was correct presumably because it was an adult's, and his was correct because the paper clip model—an appeal to physical reality—justified it.

Mat too had clever means for justifying his answers. "He explained and justified answers such as $\frac{3}{4} + \frac{1}{4} = 0$ using wooden blocks; $\frac{3}{4} + \frac{1}{4} = \frac{4}{8} = \frac{1}{2}$ by adding numbers horizontally; and $\frac{3}{4} + \frac{1}{4} = 1$ using a circle diagram. . . . The correct answer at any instance depended upon which method he had been directed to use. Thus an incorrect answer to Mat only occurred when he used a wrong method."[8]

We see then that Mat could use physical objects, diagrams, and the like to justify the results of his different methods of solution. Similarly, another child felt that this diagram (Figure 6–1) could represent $\frac{4}{8}$ or $\frac{4}{1}$ or 1.4.

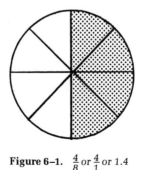

Figure 6–1. $\frac{4}{8}$ or $\frac{4}{1}$ or 1.4

While children may see mathematics as a kind of arbitrary game yielding many different answers, each can be justified in a perfectly logical way.

PATTERNS OF SUCCESS AND FAILURE

The individual child does not always succeed or always fail, and does not always use one single procedure to get these right or wrong answers. Rather, the child's answers involve complex mixtures of success and failure, and he uses several different procedures to get his answers.

At nine years, Jane was asked to do 87 + 39 and solved it as follows:

$$
\begin{array}{r}
87 \\
+\ 39 \\
\hline
15 \\
11 \\
\hline
26
\end{array}
$$

I: Maybe you can explain what is going on here. If I'm not mistaken, you've added 7 and 9. And you get?

J: 15.

I: And you add 8 and 3 and get?

J: 11 and put it right underneath and add these two together [15 and 11] and you get 26.

It is not difficult to see the strategy that Jane had used for calculation. She had (incorrectly) added the units column (7 + 9 = 15), and then added the tens column (8 + 3 = 11), placing the second sum directly beneath the first.

How did she develop this strange strategy? Since we do not know her learning history, we can only speculate. Perhaps a teacher once used a method like this to teach Jane the role of place value in addition. By this procedure, with the numbers 87 and 39, we can first add the units column, getting 16; then we add the tens column to get eleven 10's or 110. Thus:

$$
\begin{array}{r}
87 \\
+\ 39 \\
\hline
16 \\
11 \\
\hline
126
\end{array}
$$

Jane may have partially learned the teacher's method (with a crucial error in lining up the numbers), failed to understand its rationale, and simply repeated it in a blind fashion thereafter. The incorrect rule may thus have had sensible origins.

The interviewer explained Jane's mistake, and Jane then did the next problem correctly.

$$
\begin{array}{r}
46 \\
+\ 79 \\
\hline
15 \\
11 \\
\hline
125
\end{array}
$$

With big numbers, however, Jane still had problems. She did:

$$
\begin{array}{r}
1,279 \\
+\ 382 \\
\hline
11 \\
15 \\
15 \\
\hline
3,061
\end{array}
$$

After struggling with this procedure for some time, Jane said, "Maybe you're not supposed to use that method with a thousand." She then volunteered to "add it just plain," and used the traditional carrying method to get the right answer.

$$
\begin{array}{r}
1,279 \\
+\ 382 \\
\hline
1,661
\end{array}
$$

On the basis of this evidence, it seemed that Jane's use of the place value method was something of a fluke, and that she was capable of performing addition in the traditional manner. But later, Jane showed yet another method for doing addition. The interviewer asked her to add two numbers written horizontally as follows:

$$123 + 14$$

J: I don't know if I can do them that way. I can only do them on top of each other.

Smaller Numbers Can Be Harder Than Big Ones

Jane's difficulty with problems involving large numbers is entirely typical. Children often have more difficulty in applying an algorithm to larger numbers than to smaller ones. But, strangely, the difficulty does not always operate in this direction. Kathy, in the second grade, was asked to multiply 12 × 6 on paper.

K: I don't know how to do it.

I: You haven't had problems like that?

K: Yes, I've had problems like that a million times, but they have more numbers.

Kathy then demonstrated how to do 123 × 5 and got the correct answer.

I: What's the difference? This only has two numbers [referring to the 12 in the 12 × 6] and this has three [referring to the 123 in 123 × 5].

Still Kathy claimed she could not do 12 × 6. She claimed that 123 × 5 was Wynroth math—that is, the kind of math taught by the Wynroth curriculum in her school—whereas the other problem (12 × 6) was not Wynroth math. The interviewer then worked with Kathy to show her how to do multiplication with two digit numbers. After a while she concluded that 12 × 6 was also Wynroth math.

This was the first problem that she had to line up for herself. She wrote:

$$\begin{array}{r} 132 \\ \underline{14} \\ 272 \end{array}$$

So here she used a new method: lining up the numbers from left to right, and then adding in the ordinary way. Later Jane showed a variant on this procedure. After lining up the numbers from left to right, she proceeded to carry in that direction too!

Thus far, then, Jane used at least three methods for addition: the distortion of the method for demonstrating the role of place value;

the standard carrying algorithm; and the lining up on the left method.

But Jane was not satisfied with her last results. She agreed with the interviewer that "something's funny."

J: Maybe . . . it's supposed to go like this.

She wrote:

$$\begin{array}{r} 132 \\ \underline{14} \end{array}$$

J: Maybe . . . no . . . yes! That's the way it's supposed to go, because that's in the ones place, that's in the tens place, and that's in the hundreds place. We were doing it wrong.

She wrote:

$$\begin{array}{r} 132 \\ \underline{14} \\ 146 \end{array}$$

J: That looks much better.

What Jane seems to have done is this. She first recognized that the sum of 132 and 14 is not 272 as she had initially maintained, and that her left to right lining up method was therefore wrong. She tried a new method—the correct one—and realized that it was correct because it made sense in terms of the theory of place value. We shall explore the nature of such understanding below. For now, the main point is that a child exhibiting *several* wrong strategies can also understand things on a relatively deep level.

Later on, the interviewer dictated some numbers for Jane to add. She forgot her earlier insight concerning lining up numbers from right to left, and wrote:

$$\begin{array}{r} 6 \\ 79 \\ 163 \\ 940 \\ 2342 \\ \underline{15700} \end{array}$$

She indicated that she would add by carrying from left to right.

I: I'd like you to look at the numbers you have here and estimate—or guess, sort of an educated guess—as to what the sum should be when you add them all together.

Jane appeared to be thinking.

I: What seems like a reasonable number to get?

J: 17, . . . uh, . . . 18, and . . . 18,392.

I: [quite surprised] That's a pretty good guess. I mean you were pretty precise all the way to the last unit. How did you estimate that?

J: I knew that it probably would be more than seventeen hundred.

I: Seventeen hundred? Seventeen thousand I think you mean.

J: Yes, seventeen thousand, and then I just decided, I said, and just *guessed* the rest.

After all, the interviewer *had* asked her to guess.

I: How did you know that it would be more than seventeen thousand?

J: Well, that's two thousand [pointing to the 2,342] and that's fifteen thousand [15,700] which is seventeen thousand and all of this [the rest] adds up to probably more than one thousand, and I know it would probably be eighteen thousand and I just guessed the rest.

Jane's rounding procedure seems to imply a good deal of understanding of addition. Jane assumed that the two numbers that contribute most to the sum are the two largest numbers. By comparison, the other numbers are insignificant and can almost be ignored. She assumed, too, that rounding does not distort the results: in this case, one can drop the last three digits of each number without affecting the sum very substantially. Both of these assumptions—the role of the largest two numbers and the role of rounding—demonstrate at least an implicit understanding of basic aspects of addition. All this from a girl who lines up numbers and adds from left to right!

This then is Jane, the inconsistent mathematician. In the case of simple addition, she used several different calculational devices: her distortion of the place value method; lining up numbers from left to right, while adding from right to left; lining up from left to right and carrying in the same direction; and adding "regular." She was sometimes poor at adding on paper, but did an interesting mental calculation, using a rounding procedure to produce reasonably accurate

Jane's Standard Tests

What do standard tests teach us about a child like Jane? The Stanford Achievement Test showed that Jane was in the fourteenth percentile in arithmetic computations and in the sixty-eighth percentile in arithmetic concepts. There is some accuracy to this; generally Jane's concepts were more advanced than her calculations. But the picture given by standard achievement tests is too vague; it presents only the blurred outlines and fails to describe her knowledge in rich detail. The tests do not describe the strategies producing Jane's errors nor do they describe unusual competencies like her rounding procedure or application of place value theory to calculational problems. Since the test focuses only on generalities, it is of virtually no use to a teacher trying to help a child like Jane.

estimates of sums, even when very large numbers were involved. She lined up numbers incorrectly but seemed to understand something of the place value concept. *Mistakes occur for many reasons and can exist in a context of competence.*

GAPS

We have seen that side by side with the child's mistakes there exist interesting and unexpected competencies. At the same time that Jane lined up numbers incorrectly for column addition, she could make effective estimates based on sound principles. Now we shall consider more explicitly the relation between children's difficulties and their competencies. We shall see that often children who botch up standard written calculations nevertheless understand the relevant concepts on an intuitive level. They display a *gap* between written work, on the one hand, and informal methods and concepts on the other. As Freud put it (in a different context), "Perhaps there is room in the mind for opposite tendencies, for contradictions, existing side bv side."[9]

Written work and informal notions

In school, children learn standard written procedures—algorithms and other symbolic devices—that can be more powerful than what they pick up on their own. It should be easier to calculate

23 + 18 on paper than to do it mentally. But is it? Children often find written mathematics almost impossible to do and instead rely on informal counting techniques or invented strategies.

We saw that at 5–1, Court's Paul would count to a million; could add, using counters, up to 20; knew which numbers were larger than others; and was in many other ways a most precocious and competent informal mathematician. Yet Paul could not write any symbols except 1.

The teacher asked Caroline, six years of age, "If you bought twenty-four flowers and six of them were tulips and the rest were daffodils, how many daffodils would you have?"[10]

Caroline responded correctly, "eighteen."

"Now can you write down what you have done in your head?" Caroline wrote:

$$\frac{6}{24}$$

Then:

$$\begin{array}{r} 6 \\ -\ 24 \\ \hline 22 \end{array}$$

She then said, "But it ought to be eighteen, oughtn't it?"

We see then that Caroline could do a simple subtraction word problem in her head, and believed that this method gave the correct result, as indeed it did. Yet at the same time, there was no way that she could handle the problem in a formal fashion on paper.

At eight years, Alexandria could not do written division problems like $8 \div 4 = ?$, the answer to which she believed to be 1 or 0.[11] The interviewer gave Alexandria a comparable story problem. "Suppose you had eight dollars and you had four children and you wanted to share the money equally with all of the children. How much would you give to each child?"

Alexandria repeating the problem, mistakenly said, "Suppose you had five dollars . . .," but then proceeded to solve it: "a dollar and twenty-five cents."

So Alexandria was helpless when asked to divide with *written* numerals. At the same time, she was adept at solving analogous story problems.

Paul, six years of age, had been standing by, listening to the interview with Alexandria. After hearing the story problem, he proceeded to invent story problems for addition, subtraction, and multiplication. For example; "Three threes would be like if you had three bags, and there were three things in each bag."

And: "Three minus two would be like you had three dollars and you gave away two. You'd have *one* left."

The important part about this observation is that Paul could not read or write simple arithmetic like $3 - 2 = 1$, or $3 \times 3 = 9$. In his case, the gap between written and story arithmetic was extreme. He was helpless with written numerals but facile with spoken, concrete problems, which he could create and solve mentally.

Of course there are exceptions. Some children are comfortable with algorithms and use them spontaneously. Trika, a third grader, provides a dramatic example of what is apparently a rarity.[12] The interviewer asked how many pennies there would be altogether if she had sixteen pennies in one hand and ten in the other. Trika got the right answer. Asked how she did it, she answered that she had imagined the written numbers

$$\begin{array}{r} 16 \\ + 10 \\ \hline \end{array}$$

and then computed mentally in this way: "6 and no number, there are 6; you add these here [1 and 1] and get 2. So 26." Trika had pictured the written problem in her head and solved it mentally!

Unfortunately, more typical than Trika are children who experience considerable difficulty with standard computation. They fail in school, are far behind their classmates, and are considered to have low mathematical aptitude. Yet we shall see that these children too possess informal competencies of some power.

Vivian, a fifth grader, was identified by her teacher as a child with severe learning problems; she was at least a year and a half behind in her work.[13] Nevertheless, she was adept at using counting strategies to solve simple computational problems. Given two numbers to add, she would typically count on from the larger to achieve a correct result.

At the same time, she found written numbers harder to deal with. For example, she was shown fifteen dots (three rows of five each) and asked to write down the number. She counted the dots, one by one, and wrote the correct total. Next she was shown twenty-five dots in another collection, counted them, and wrote down the total below the 15. How many altogether? She looked at the numbers she had written, counted on her fingers, and wrote 13. She had simply added all the individual digits (1 + 5 + 2 + 5), a strategy that is not entirely uncommon. Written arithmetic, as Vivian practiced it, revealed that the sum of two collections is less than either taken separately!

Yet Vivian had no difficulty dealing with real objects. The interviewer asked her to work with the dots.

> I: Thirteen? You had twenty-five dots here, and fifteen here, and if we put them all together, how many would we have?

Vivian looked at the twenty-five dot array and said, "twenty-five." Then she pointed to each member of the fifteen dot array, and counted on, "twenty-six, twenty-seven, . . . forty."

So given concrete objects to work with (the dots), Vivian used a sensible strategy to get an accurate result; given written numbers (which described the objects she had just counted!), she used a bizarre procedure to get a wrong result. The gap between Vivian's informal and formal knowledge was extreme. The interviewer then tried to get Vivian's judgment concerning which answer was really correct. Vivian had so little confidence in her counting methods that she said she did not know.

Ralph, an eleven-year-old fifth grader working about two years below grade level, showed a similar gap between written work and informal knowledge. Indeed, his informal skills were impressive. Given collections of objects to add (for example, twenty-three pennies and eighteen pennies), he would group the objects and count by fives or tens. He solved mental problems by clever regrouping strategies. For example, to add 75 + 58, "I took the 70 and 50, counted by tens and that made 120. Then I took the 5 from the 75 and that made 125. From the 8, I took 5 more for 130 and 3 more is 133." He could add up to three digit numbers in his head in this manner. He was also adept at subtraction involving real objects and mental subtraction: in both cases he used grouping or regrouping strategies.

At the same time, Ralph's written computations were seriously in error. He lined up numbers from left to right, as in $\begin{array}{r} 23 \\ + 5 \\ \hline 19 \end{array}$. He did not know how to carry. For example, given $\begin{array}{r} 73 \\ + 16 \\ \hline \end{array}$ he began to add from the left, doing 1 + 1 = 2. Next he did 9 + 6 = 15, which would have given $\dfrac{\begin{array}{r}19\\16\end{array}}{215}$. But somehow—how is not clear—he realized that 215 contained too many digits. His solution was simply to ignore the 5! This then gave an answer of 21. In the case of subtraction, he was asked to do $15 - 7$ on paper (he had already obtained the correct answer in his head) and wrote $\dfrac{\begin{array}{r}15\\-\ 7\end{array}}{65}$. After having lined up the num-

bers incorrectly, he used the common method of subtracting the smaller number from the larger.

We see then that Ralph was skilled at arithmetic except when he had to do it on paper. According to Russell, "Ralph would never work problems on paper, unless I told him to do so. And wildly contradictory answers didn't bother Ralph in the least. He seemed to believe that one gets different answers when problems are worked out on paper, rather than in an informal way, and that both procedures are correct. When I asked Ralph which answer is right, he said 'both.' And when I asked why, he said 'It's different.' "[14] For Ralph, written work and informal procedures are separate, but equal. Often when such a gap exists, the child does not know which is right and which is wrong.

The origin of the gap

Why do children have so much difficulty with written mathematics? Perhaps part of the answer is this. As we have seen, children's early and self-invented arithmetic mainly involves counting procedures applied to real objects. They usually count on their fingers to get a sum. Methods like this work easily and well. Next children are taught various written procedures for accomplishing the same purposes. Unfortunately, they often fail to understand the necessity or rationale for written methods. Nevertheless, they are imposed on them and in school they are required to use them. The result is not only a bizarre written arithmetic, but a gap between it and children's informal knowledge.

At 6–2, Rebecca was doing some addition problems. The interviewer asked, "Suppose you have twenty oranges and Debbie has thirteen oranges. How many oranges are there all together?"

Rebecca used some small blocks to solve the problem. First she tried to count out twenty blocks to represent one set and thirteen blocks to represent the other. Then she combined the two sets of blocks, and counted the conglomerate to reach a total of 35. Although she made a few counting errors, she had a clear, consistent and sensible approach to addition problems: represent each set with the appropriate number of objects and count the total.

Next the interviewer wrote some symbols on paper. She asked Rebecca to add 3 + 15. Rebecca looked at the numbers, pointed to each, and said, "three." The interviewer was surprised. Why does 3 + 15 equal 3? Rebecca again counted the numbers (ignoring the plus). The sum is 3, she indicated, because there are three numerals.

For Rebecca, then, the way to do addition is to count the objects representing members of a set. Blocks can represent members of a set and so can numerals. Each numeral, regardless of what it is, represents a member of a set. And to get the sum, one merely counts up the number of numerals!

Probably not many children do exactly what Rebecca did. But that is not the point of the observation. Rebecca's behavior highlights the difficulties many children have in working with written arithmetic. Before learning to read and understand written numerals—mathematical symbols—Rebecca had already developed for the purpose of addition various counting strategies, involving real objects. She was adept at finding the sum when real objects were involved. Then symbols were introduced—not by Rebecca but by a teacher or a parent—and Rebecca had to make sense of them. But doing so is a very difficult process and Rebecca had trouble with it. She tried to understand the symbols by assimilating them into what she already knew, namely, the counting of objects. Thus, she mistakenly counted the numerals just as she had counted the blocks.

So before encountering written mathematics, children invent sensible methods for dealing with arithmetic problems in the real world. Then written symbolism—those strange marks on paper—is introduced and children need help in interpreting it. They need to see the connection between what they can already do and the arbitrary symbols. They have to learn the meaning of symbols—that is, how symbolism relates to previously developed knowledge.

Diana, a third grader, showed another kind of confusion concerning written symbols. She was asked to add thirty-six dots to thirteen dots arrayed as in Figure 6–2. She did this successfully by using a counting method: she started with 36 and counted on 13

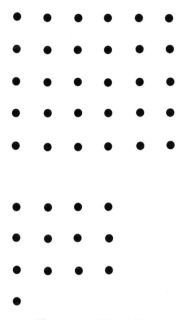

Figure 6–2.   *Diana's Dots*

more to reach 49. Then the interviewer asked her to demonstrate on paper. She wrote:

$$
\begin{array}{r}
666 \\
666 \\
444 \\
+\ 1 \\
\hline
\end{array}
$$

and added the numbers, using a carrying method.

Why did Diana write the numbers in this fashion? She was trying to make a kind of map. She saw that there were six here, six here, and six here, and so she wrote 666. Under this method, three groups of six dots became 666 or six hundred and sixty-six. Diana confused a numerical map of the dots with a computational formula. And when she added up her map, she got a strange result.

We see then that Diana had some appreciation of written symbolism. She knew that numbers could be used to represent groups of objects, but she did not understand how to use those numbers to calculate. While she easily used finger counting to combine objects, she was not skilled at combining numbers in the process of calculation. Unlike Rebecca, she did not simply count up the number of written numbers. She tried to use a carrying method, but she used it on the wrong numbers. She tried to perform calculations on a map. (This is somewhat like going down route 9 if the map says to start on route 6 and then go to route 3.) While Diana knew what each symbol represented separately, she needed to learn how to manipulate them to get a sum. The process of learning written arithmetic is a long one.

Eventually, the child learns to perform written calculations correctly, but their full significance is not immediately clear. Thus Kathy, a second grader, first added thirty-six dots to thirteen dots by a counting method to get the correct answer. Then the interviewer instructed her to add 36 + 13 on paper. She had no idea as to what the sum would be. She struggled through the calculation, adding from left to right, but eventually got the correct answer. The interviewer then asked Kathy if the written method represented another useful way of adding thirty-six and thirteen dots. At first she denied it, saying that she still had to "count in my head." But then the relevance of the written method dawned on her. She said with surprise, "Yeah, you could do it this way. You could put 36 down and you could put this number down and put a line and then you'd find the answer!"

Often, it seems that children are comfortable with the uses of informal counting methods to solve problems; at the same time, they learn to perform written calculations as a kind of isolated exercise or game, and all too rarely do they learn the meaning of the calculations by connecting the game with what they already know.

SUMMARY

Typically children's errors are based on systematic rules. They make errors because they add sideways or always subtract the smaller number from the larger (forgetting to borrow). Errors are seldom capricious or random. Often children think of mathematics as an isolated game with peculiar sets of rules and no evident relation to reality. At the same time, children's faulty rules have sensible origins. Usually they are a distortion or misinterpretation of sound procedures.

Individual children can display extraordinary inconsistency in mathematical behavior. The child may show unusual combinations of strengths and weaknesses, of effective computational approaches and bizarre procedures.

There often exist gaps between children's informal knowledge and their written work. In general, children are uncomfortable with written work and botch it up. At the same time they may possess an impressive informal understanding of the same concepts. Even children with severe learning problems may have unsuspected informal strengths. The gap may originate because instruction does not devote sufficient attention to integrating formal written procedures with children's already existing and relatively powerful informal knowledge.

PRINCIPLES

1. *Errors result from organized strategies and rules.* Children's behavior is meaningful, not capricious. There is usually a reason for their mistakes, and the reason is a systematic rule. Most often it does not help to think of errors in terms of "low IQ" or "learning disabilities." These labels are too general for the purposes of sound teaching. The use of such vague labels conveys the false impression of having explained something while they merely serve to distract attention from the real problem—children's faulty rules and the gaps between their formal and informal knowledge.

2. *The faulty rules underlying errors have sensible origins.* Children do not construct faulty rules because they are ornery or stupid. Rather they are derivations from what they have been taught. Of course, the derivations are objectively illogical and wrong; but psychologically they make some sense to the child.

3. *Too often children see arithmetic as an activity isolated from their ordinary concerns.* They see mathematics as a kind of game with its own unique rules, unrelated to any other activity.

4. *Children demonstrate a gap between informal and formal knowledge.* For them, written mathematics *is* a game. They do not relate it to their already existing informal knowledge of mathematics.

5. *Children often possess unsuspected strengths.* While they make many errors in written arithmetic, children may in fact possess relatively powerful informal knowledge. This can be used as the basis for effective instruction.

Chapter 7

Learning Difficulties

This chapter examines in detail four children experiencing severe difficulties in the learning of arithmetic. I try to show how the principles discussed in preceding chapters can be used to understand these children and help them to learn.

Three of the children (Bob, Patty, and Stacy) were selected in this way: I asked a third grade teacher in an elementary school serving both middle- and lower-class children in Ithaca, New York, to choose the students having the most trouble in arithmetic. I wanted to know nothing about them except that they were having considerable difficulties learning arithmetic. I did not want to be told their test scores, their IQs, their home situations, or anything else. I did not want myself or the other interviewers to be biased in any way; we wanted to discover the child's weaknesses—and strengths—for ourselves, by our own methods of informal interviewing.* While I requested no information, the teacher could not keep from telling us that all of these children suffered from perceptual problems. At the time, there seemed to be a virtual epidemic of this disease in the Ithaca schools. No doubt it has lately been supplanted by something else. Finally, George was selected when a parent asked for help with her child.

The children were receiving an eclectic form of instruction. For example, Patty sometimes worked in her classroom on Suppes's *Sets and Numbers* text. As the name suggests, this is a new math approach, based heavily on set theory and logic. Sometimes she went to the learning center where she worked on a programmed learning system. This involved a procedure that attempted first to diagnose children's level of arithmetic knowledge and then assigned them to

---

*Bob was interviewed by Anita Levy, Patty and Stacy by Barbara Allardice and myself, and George by Lynn De Jonghe. The first three sets of interviews were recorded on video tape; the last on audio tape.

specific lessons that they had to get right before being sent on to the next topic.

Consider now four ordinary children doing badly in school.

BOB AND GEORGE

Bob, a fifth grader, exhibits a pattern that seems typical of children experiencing difficulties in school mathematics. Like Ralph, discussed in the last chapter, Bob had trouble with standard written algorithms, but at the same time possessed effective informal procedures. There was a profound gap between his formal and informal knowledge.[1]

Consider first his work in addition.

I: Now we'll do some written problems. How much is 8 plus 11?

B: [He wrote 8 + 11 = 19.] 19.

I: How did you do it?

B: I counted. Just take the largest number and add on 8.

I: So you went: 11, 12, 13 . . . ?

B: Yeah.

Bob had used the common strategy of counting on from the largest number, and could even describe his method in words.

I: What about 22 plus 19?

B: [He wrote 22 + 19.] 41?

I: Did you count from 22 by ones?

B: I took the 10 and that's 32, and then I took the 9, and that's 41.

Bob had used regrouping to facilitate his addition. He rearranged the problem into (22 + 10) + 9. He knew immediately that 22 + 10 = 32 and then added on the 9.

In the same way, when given 22 + 26, he did (22 + 20) + 6. "I added the 20, got 42; then took 6 and added it." We see that Bob used sensible, economical methods to do simple addition. From his performance to this point, he does not seem to suffer from fundamental difficulties in understanding arithmetic.

The interviewer then wanted to see if he could do standard written problems like

$$\begin{array}{r} 158 \\ 265. \\ + 98 \\ \hline \end{array}$$

As we saw in the last chapter, Bob had trouble with problems like this.

I: Can you do this problem with carrying?

He began by adding 8 + 5 + 8 to get 21. He wrote:

$$1\overset{1}{5}8$$
$$265$$
$$\underline{98}$$
$$2$$

B: I take the 2 and write it down here [in the units column] and carry the 1 . . . I carried, so I put the big number down here."

Bob's rule was always to carry the smaller of the two numbers obtained by adding the units column. Although this rule has sensible origins, it leads to consistently wrong answers.

Given 18 + 5, he did:

^{318}
$$\underline{+\ 5}$$
$$41$$

He got 8 + 5 = 13, put down the 1 in the units column, and carried the 3.

I: Do you think that's the right answer?
B: Yeah.
I: If you had eighteen candies and you got five more, how many would you have altogether?
B: [He counted on his fingers] 18, 19, 20, 21, 22, 23. [Then he looked at his previous answer, 41.] That's wrong!

Unlike many other children, Bob placed greater confidence in his informal, finger counting method than he did in the written algorithm. He relied on his own intuition, rather than on his misinterpretation of what had been taught in school.

Bob's work with subtraction showed a similar gap between informal and formal knowledge.

I: Do you want to write a take-away problem for yourself?

B: [He wrote 9 ÷ 5 = .] 4?

I: Right. How did you do it?

B: I counted backwards.

The gap is evident at the outset: Bob could not write a proper symbol for minus; and at the same time he solved the problem by a sound informal procedure, namely counting backwards.

As in the case of addition, he used a regrouping procedure when the numbers were relatively large.

I: If you had ninety-eight dollars and you gave away twenty-nine, how many would you have left?

B: OK. 88, 78, and 9 would be 67.

I: Almost.

B: I mean 69.

Bob had transformed 98 − 29 into [(98 − 10) − 10] − 9. He first subtracted or counted back by tens—98, 88, 78—and then counted back by ones to subtract the final 9. At first he made a minor error in the last step, but he soon corrected it.

Asked to do written subtraction, Bob did poorly.

I: If you had 158 and you took away 96, how many would you have left?

Bob wrote

$$\begin{array}{r} 158 \\ 96 \\ \hline \end{array}$$

Then he corrected it to

$$\begin{array}{r} 158 \\ \underline{96} \\ \end{array}$$

He did 8 minus by 6 by counting backward from 8. Then he said, "9 minus 5 is 4." This gave him

$$\begin{array}{r} 158 \\ \underline{96} \\ 142 \end{array}$$

Next the interviewer gave him a simpler problem.

I: Let's see, now, 21 take away 5.

Bob did

$$
\begin{array}{r}
21 \\
-\ 5 \\
\hline
24
\end{array}
$$

I: Do you think that's the right answer?

B: [He checked his work.] Yes.

I: If you had twenty-one candies and gave away five, how many would you have left?

B: Oh! I think I added.

He seemed to mean that since he got more than 21 he must have added.

I: Do you still think that's the right answer?

B: No. 'Cause five take away from 21 is 16.

I: [He pointed to his written 21 − 5 = 24.] But why isn't that the right answer?

B: I don't know.

I: You had 21 and you took away 5, and you had 24 left. What's wrong with that?

B: Oh! I know! It's from this one [the 1 in 21] that it was supposed to be taken away from.

In other words, Bob recognized that he should have subtracted the 5 from the 1 rather than the 1 from the 5.

In brief, Bob first used an incorrect written procedure for subtraction. This gave him 21 − 5 = 24, where the result is larger than the number he started with. He could easily do the same problem in his head by counting backwards and in this way got the right answer. Bob then realized that his written answer was wrong. "Oh! I think I added." This shows that he knew that in subtraction you should end up with less, not more, than you started with. Then he saw why he was wrong in the first place: he had reversed the order of subtraction.

George, a fifth grader too, was also typical in displaying a gap between informal and formal knowledge.[2]

After investigating George's counting, the interviewer said, "Now I'm going to give you some arithmetic questions. You write them down yourself. How much is 4 plus 2?"

George wrote: $4 \times 2 - 8$.

The interviewer thought that perhaps he did not understand the word plus.

I: How much is 3 *and* 1?

George wrote: $3 \times 1 - 3$.

I: How much is 3 and 4 more altogether?

George wrote $3 \times 4 = $, and then hesitated.

I: Perhaps you could figure this out another way. Would using these clips help?

George took three paper clips, then another four, and counted them all to get the correct answer of 7.

I: O.K. Now try writing this one: 5 and 2.

George wrote: $5 \times 2 = 10$.

I: What happens if you do it the other way?

George took five paper clips, then two, and counted to get 7.

George's responses illustrate a dramatic gap between the informal and formal. Given a spoken addition problem (5 and 2), George used either informal counting to get a correct answer or formal written multiplication to get a wrong one. In his informal mode of operation, he used concrete aids, counting and combining paper clips. In the formal mode, he converted the spoken addition problem into the corresponding multiplication formula and in general (with the exception of 3×4, which he did not complete) solved it. A strange gap indeed.

The cases of Bob and George illustrate some very fundamental points, which we stress even at the risk of repetition.

1. The child's errors often derive from systematic but incorrect written procedures. In adding, Bob always carried the smaller

number; in subtracting, he always subtracted the smaller number. Both methods are systematic but wrong. Neither is capricious nor random. In adding, George always multiplied on paper. Again, wrong but systematic.

2. The child often possesses sound informal techniques for arithmetic. Bob and George added by counting and by regrouping. Bob subtracted by counting backward. These informal techniques led to correct answers.

3. There often exists a gap between the child's informal and formal knowledge. Using formal, school-derived techniques, both Bob and George did poorly; relying on informal knowledge, they did well.

4. Understanding a child's methods for doing arithmetic often leads to suggestions for helping him. Since Bob's informal counting methods were powerful, and since he himself placed confidence in them, they could serve as a useful basis for instruction. For example, Bob spontaneously made use of regrouping. Given 22 + 19, he regrouped into (22 + 10) + 9. This informal knowledge could be used to teach the standard carrying algorithm. The latter regroups 22 + 19 into (20 + 10) + (2 + 9), which is not very much different from Bob's invented method. Similarly, George could be taught addition through counting. *School mathematics should be built on the child's intuitions.*

PATTY

Patty, a nine-year-old, illustrates another kind of difficulty. She was first given a subtraction problem, which she did correctly by using the standard algorithm with borrowing. She wrote:

$$9\ ^5\not{6}\ ^12$$
$$-\ 4\ \ 3\ \ 9$$
$$\overline{5\ \ 2\ \ 3}$$

The she did an addition problem correctly $\begin{array}{r} 226 \\ +\ 421 \\ \hline 647 \end{array}$. Again, she

used the standard method, except that her procedure was to count out loud and on her fingers when she could not remember the relevant number facts. Thus, she added from right to left, remembering that 2 and 2 are 4 and counting to determine that 4 and 2 are 6.

Next she did $\overset{1}{\underset{68}{+\ 39}}$ 29. Again this involved the standard algorithm, with carrying, and was done in part by counting on the fingers. Patty could give no rationale for the carrying of the 1. Her only response was that it was wrong to place the 1 on the bottom with the 6 and the 8.

These first few incidents show that Patty had a few basic skills. She was familiar with the common borrowing and carrying methods for subtraction and addition, respectively. She could execute these fairly smoothly, at least under certain conditions—specifically, when relatively small numbers, each having the same number of digits, were involved, and when she could count on her fingers and therefore did not have to rely on memory for number facts. She showed one common and minor weakness: she did not seem to know much about the theory of place value and hence could not *explain* why one carries, although she could do it.

So far it did not seem if Patty had any particular difficulties—perceptual or otherwise—with arithmetic. But, as we have seen before, for example in considering Jane's inconsistency, the child often displays a complex pattern of skills and weaknesses.

I: I'm going to give you another problem. You seem to be doing pretty well adding. Suppose you have 29 again and 4.

Patty wrote: $\underset{}{\overset{29}{+\ 4}}$.

Before placing the 4 under the 2 her hand hesitated under the 9; apparently she could not decide where to place the 4. Patty then said, "You put the 4 over here . . . that would be . . . that's 9 . . . [she whispered] 2, 3, 4, 5, 6 . . . 69." She had counted to get the sum of 2 and 4. She wrote $\underset{69}{\overset{29}{+\ 4}}$.

I: What does it say right here?

P: 29 and 4.

I: Are how much?

P: 69.

This was Patty's first error in the interview. She got a wrong result (69) because she employed a wrong strategy. When there were unequal numbers of digits she lined them up from left to right and then applied the standard addition algorithm, with counting on the fingers, from right to left. This systematic but incorrect strategy, which we have seen in other children, leads to predictable errors.

At this point, one might wish to intervene and straighten out Patty's incorrect method. But there was still much to learn about her.

I: You're sure that 29 and 4 are 69?

P: Altogether?

I: Altogether.

P: No.

I: How much are 29 and 4?

Patty made a large number of tallies on the bottom of the page. She appeared to count them, at least sometimes using her fingers. Then she announced the result: 33.

This seemed to show a gap between sound informal methods and faulty formal ones. Patty had an incorrect strategy for written addition, as described above. At the same time, she had an effective strategy for performing addition when real objects—here tallies—are involved. The correct strategy for objects is essentially to combine the two groups and count the aggregate. There is a gap between written work and arithmetic with real objects.

The interviewer wanted to determine whether Patty placed more confidence in the written procedure than in the counting one.

I: 33. O.K. How come this says 69 [she pointed to the written work]?

P: Ooops! Because you're not doing it like that [she pointed to the tallies]. Oh, this [the 69] is wrong.

Apparently Patty saw that her answer of 69 was wrong, and that it differed from that result obtained by counting. She changed the 69 to 33. Patty seemed to have greater confidence in her informal method than in written addition.

At this point, the interviewer decided to challenge Patty's new response (33) in order to see how firm was her belief in the counting-derived result.

I: How can you put a 3 here [referring to the second 3 in 33] if it says 9 here [referring to the 9 in 29]?

Patty looked at what was written
$$\begin{array}{r} 29 \\ + \ 4 \\ \hline 33 \end{array}$$
and changed it back to
$$\begin{array}{r} 29 \\ + \ 4 \\ \hline 69 \end{array}$$.

P: That's 9 and that's gotta be 6. It's just that you're doing it differently than that.

I: So you get a different answer.

P: Yeah. 'Cause you're adding all of this up together [meaning the tallies]. You're not adding it all up altogether this way [she pointed to the written work]. You're putting the 9 by itself and that's 69.

I: So when you do it on paper you get 69 and if you do it with the little marks you get how many?

P: 33. Because you're adding all of it altogether. And you're not doing it over here.

For Patty, written work was a world apart from the addition of real objects.

I: Suppose we had 29 of these little chips and put out 4 more. Would we get 33 or 69?

P: 33.

I: How do you know?

P: Because I did it down here and I added 4 more onto it [she pointed to the tallies on the bottom of the page].

I: O.K. So that means these chips would be like these lines.

P: Yes.

I: What would be another thing that would be like this [the written problem] where I could get 69?

P: There ain't no other way, I don't think.

So Patty knew that several ways of counting objects (tallies, chips) were equivalent, but could think of nothing real that corresponded to the written problem.

I: Let's see. You have 29 and 4 and you get 69. Suppose you had 30, so you had 1 more here, and 3, so you have 1 less there. Would you still get 69?

The interviewer's intention was to present Patty with a situation producing a contradiction. 30 + 3 should yield the same sum as 29 + 4. Patty should easily see that 30 had 1 more than 29, but 3 had 1 less than 4. Yet by Patty's method, she should get a different result

for $\begin{array}{r} 29 \\ + 4 \\ \hline \end{array}$ than $\begin{array}{r} 30 \\ + 3 \\ \hline \end{array}$. Would Patty see the contradiction?

P: No. You'd get bigger than 69.

She did 30 + 4 instead of 30 + 3 and wrote $\begin{array}{r} 30 \\ + 4 \\ \hline 70 \end{array}$.

. P: Yep. I told you you'd get more than 69.

At this point, it seems clear that Patty has been using two separate methods: a combining and counting method to get correct sums when real objects are involved and an incorrect written algorithm—lining up on the left with uneven numbers of digits—when written numbers are involved. Now the interviewer wondered whether Patty would continue to employ her written method in extreme cases.

I: O.K. Let me try something, Patty. Can you write down for me 100 plus 1?

Patty wrote $\begin{array}{r} 100 \\ + 1 \\ \hline 200 \end{array}$ and said, "Zero, zero, and 2. It would be 200."

I: 100 plus 1, huh? Do you think that's right? Got any other way of doing it?

P: No. Unless the 1 is on the wrong side. Unless the 1 is supposed to be there [she pointed to the ones column].

I: Where's the 1 supposed to be?

P: I think it's supposed to be there [pointed to the hundreds column].

I: You think it's supposed to be there, huh? O.K. Let's do another one. What about 10 plus 1?

Patty wrote $\begin{array}{r} 10 \\ + 1 \\ \hline 20 \end{array}$ and said, "That's zero and that's 2. 20."

I: 20, think that's right?

P: Yeah.

I: Got any other way of doing it?

Patty indicated no.

At this point, it was clear that Patty's written method generalized widely, even to extreme cases like 100 + 1. Now the interviewer wanted to get Patty to see the discrepancy between her written and counting methods.

I: Well, suppose you couldn't use paper at all and I said how much is 10 plus 1?

P: I'd count on my fingers.

I: Why don't you do it?

Patty held up all ten fingers and stared at them.

P: You have 10 [she looked at the fingers]. You put the zero on the bottom [draws a zero with her finger].

I: Just use your fingers now.

P: Then you put 2 and you add 1 and 1 and it's 2.

Patty seemed unable to count 10 on her fingers! Instead she persisted in using the written procedure, apparently doing in her head something very much like $\begin{array}{r} 10 \\ +\ 1 \\ \hline 20 \end{array}$.

I: What about on your fingers? Show me how you do it on your fingers. You can use my fingers too. Put out your fingers too.

P: You put the zero on.

I: No, I don't see any zeros. All I see are these little fingers. Never mind zeros.

P: That's hard. [She looked as though thinking intently.]

I: Now you have all kinds of fingers to work with, Patty. Now you figure out how much is 10 plus 1.

P: You have to put a zero underneath.

I: I don't see any zero at all. All I see are these fingers.

P: O.K. If you want zero you have to take those ten away [she pointed to the interviewer's fingers]. You put zero, then you have 1 and 1 left and you add them up and you get 2. So it's 20.

I: Can you do it without zeros?

P: No.

Patty was most persistent. She could not seem to get away from using the incorrect written algorithm, even when finger counting was suggested.

I: How about with little marks on your paper like you did here? How can you make 10 and 1 on the paper?

In other words, could Patty use tallies to solve the problem of 10 and 1? Patty made ten tallies.

P: [She whispered] 1, 2 . . . 10, and then you put 1 [she made another mark].

I: How many do you have altogether?

P: 11.

She made a sweeping motion with her hand as if to indicate that she meant to combine the two sets.

I: 11.

P: Yeah. Altogether.

This incident seemed to show once again that Patty used one procedure (the incorrect algorithm) for written numbers and even fingers and another procedure (combining and counting) for tallies. The gap between the two seemed considerable. On the other hand, there was something strange going on with the word *altogether*.

I: Eleven altogether . . . Let's do this . . . There are 10 of these [chips] and here's 1 more. How many do you think altogether?

P: Altogether, it would be 11.

I: O.K. What about 10 *plus* one, not *altogether*, but *plus*?

P: Then you'd have to put 20.

This was very interesting indeed. Even when real objects were involved, Patty responded to the word *plus* with her incorrect algorithm. And she used the sensible procedure of combining and counting only when the word *altogether* was used. What would she do if written numbers were used?

I: What if we write down on paper, here's 20, now I write down another 1, and you want to find out how much the 20 and 1 are altogether.

The interviewer wrote 20 1 placing the numbers side by side. He had used the word *altogether,* which should help her.

P: It's 21.

I: O.K. Now what would 20 *plus* 1 be? [The interviewer pointed at the written numbers.]

P: 20 *plus* 1? $\left[\text{She wrote } \begin{array}{r} 20 \\ + \ 1 \\ \hline 30 \end{array} \ . \right]$

The interviewer's first interpretation was wrong. It was not true that Patty used the counting strategy with real objects and the incorrect algorithm with written numbers. Unlike many other children, Patty did not simply show a gap between her informal methods and her written arithmetic. Instead, matters were far more complex. For Patty, language was crucial. Given the word *plus,* she applied an incorrect addition method to both objects and written numbers. Given *altogether,* she used a sensible counting procedure, again for both objects and written numbers. *Altogether* is a natural word for addition: Patty probably used it in everyday life to talk about adding things. *Plus* is a school word that Patty seems to have associated with a wrong algorithm that she did not understand.

The case study of Patty teaches us several things.

1. As we have seen over and over again, a child's mistakes are seldom capricious; they are instead the result of systematic but wrong strategies. Patty got wrong answers because she lined up numbers from left to right when the word *plus* was used.

2. The artificial (albeit carefully defined) language of mathematics can present the child with considerable difficulties. *Plus, congruent, minus,* and the like are unfamiliar words that children frequently misunderstand. Defining the artificial words does not guarantee comprehension. The statement that subtraction is a binary operation or a relation among ordered pairs may be crucial for the mathematician but of little help for the child. Perhaps a greater effort could be made to relate the artificial terms to the child's familiar words like *take away* and *altogether.*

3. The child often displays unsuspected strengths. There were several things Patty could do quite well. Despite frequent failure in

school, she could add correctly when she used her informal counting strategy. It is crucial to locate areas of strength in the problem child. Apparently, Patty's teacher was either unaware of her strengths or was unable to exploit them.

4. The *individual's* particular constellation of difficulties often takes a unique form. Patty's problem with *plus* was unusual. This very uniqueness leads to doubts about the value of standard tests. It is hard to see how they can be sufficiently sensitive to subtleties of this type. In addition to standard tests—and perhaps *instead* of them—we require flexible techniques for interviewing individual children.

5. Sound knowledge of children's difficulties leads to ways of helping them. The teacher could try to help Patty by making the connection between her word *altogether* and the arithmetic word *plus*. Also, the teacher might assist Patty by building on her strength—the counting and combining strategy. Instead of merely *telling* her to line up numbers differently, the teacher might help her to see that her "altogether strategy" makes sense, and that it is related to the written algorithm. If Patty could be led to see how the written algorithm is in some ways equivalent to combining and counting on, then perhaps she could learn to appreciate why one needs to line up numbers properly in the algorithm.

STACY

Stacy, also a third grader, seemed almost retarded at the outset.

I: Can you tell me first what kind of work you are doing in math now?

Stacy responded, and continued to respond throughout the session, in a slow, quiet voice. Her manner was extremely diffident—even lethargic and depressed.

S: Lots of things.
I: You write stuff on paper. Can you show me what stuff you write?
S: Papers like math [she then began to write a sentence in words as well as numerals].
I: Can you read that?
S: Jimmy had 8 cats; he gave Brian 2 cats.
I: What comes next?

S: How many does Jimmy have?

I: How many do you think he has?

S: 5.

I: How did you know that?

S: He had 8, and 2 and 1.

It was very hard to get Stacy to respond—to indicate how she had done the problem.

I: How did you do that, Stacy? He had eight cats, and he gave Brian two cats. How many did he have left?

S: 5. He had 5 and 2 others got away.

I: So how many did he have left?

S: Eight cats and I count back.

I: How do you count back?

S: 8 and I got 3 more and then I took 2 away.

I: What do you mean 3 more? Let's start from the beginning. Show me how you count back.

S: 8, 7, 6, 5, 4. He had 4 left.

I: How did you know to stop at 4? You went 8, 7, 6, 5, 4. How did you know to stop at 4?

S: Because there's 7.

This initial episode gives the flavor of interaction with Stacy. She posed herself a very simple problem with which a third grader ought to have no difficulty. Indeed, the problem was in words, rather than written numerals, and involved a simple story: If Jimmy had eight cats and gave away two, how many would be left? In response to this problem, Stacy did several things. The most obvious is that she gave several *different* wrong answers. She changed her response several times. She indicated that her method of solution was by counting backwards. But her behavior did not seem to be a simple product of this or any other strategy. Indeed, her responses were so disorganized and chaotic that it is hard to see how any underlying rules could have produced them. In brief, Stacy gave wrong answers to an extremely simple problem and seemed to have no organized method for producing answers.

The remainder of the first interview showed that Stacy's work was on a very low level. The interviewer gave her a very simple problem: If there were four dogs and two ran away, how many would be left? Stacy gave the correct answer. When asked how she did it, she replied, "Because 2 and 2 is 4." So Stacy seemed to do subtraction by remembering some relevant addition facts. Asked to solve this problem by counting backwards, she could not do so: she merely persisted in the addition or produced apparently chaotic, senseless behavior.

Next, the interviewer gave Stacy some simple addition problems. First, "How much are three apples and four apples?" Stacy answered, 6 "because 3 and 4 is 6." The wrong answer was apparently the result of faulty memory of the addition facts. Asked to do the problem by counting, Stacy merely shrugged her shoulder and shook her head—behaviors that she often displayed when she did not know what to do. Next the interviewer asked Stacy, "How much are two oranges and one more?" She got the answer right, apparently because she remembered the number facts. That was the end of the first interview.

Stacy could do very little. She was struggling with problems that should have been trivially simple for a child her age. Her only achievement was occasionally to remember some number facts. She seemed unable to use counting procedures—which, as we have seen, are usually children's method of preference.

After the first interview, we were very discouraged. We seemed to have encountered a child—the first we had seen—who had almost nothing going for her. The initial episode led us to formulate the following questions: Is she retarded? Can she hear properly? Was she very nervous or intimidated by the interviewer? Can she count? Can she conserve number? How would she do with concrete objects? Some of the questions referred to her motivation and some to her intellectual abilities. We wanted to know, essentially, whether the testing situation failed to uncover her true competence or whether she had much of any competence to begin with.

In the next session, the interviewer first established that Stacy could count as high as 80. Also, Stacy could solve Piaget's conservation problem: she recognized that a row of seven elements had the same number as another row of seven, regardless of whether the rows were the same length or whether one was bunched up.

Then the interviewer asked Stacy to get seven chips from a large pile of chips. Stacy took seven, one at a time, and put them in a straight line. The interviewer asked her to get three more. Stacy did so, putting them in a line below the first. Thus:

Figure 7–1. *Stacy's chips*

I: O.K. How many do you have altogether now?

S: Ten.

I: Ten. Very good. How did you figure that out?

S: Just counted them.

I: Counted them up. O.K. Now suppose we have one more. Can you get one more chip? How many do we have altogether now?

S: Eleven.

I: Eleven. And how about one more. How many do we have now?

S: Twelve.

I: How come you did that so fast?

S: There's 11, then I count 12.

I: You count 12. O.K. How about getting two more?

S: [quickly] 14.

I: 14. O.K. How are you doing that so fast? What are you doing in your head? Are you doing something, saying some numbers to yourself?

S: I say 13, 14, like that.

Stacy could count collections of objects; she could remember from one situation to the next; she could add by counting on when real objects are involved and when the numbers are small. Stacy had stopped shrugging her shoulders; she looked more lively. Later in the interview she demonstrated an ability to work with larger numbers. She was able to add ten and twelve chips.

Next, the interviewer wanted to see if Stacy could do addition in the absence of real objects. The interviewer took four chips, one at a time, and placed them behind a screen. The interviewer did the same with another three chips, and said that there are three chips behind the screen here and four there. All Stacy could see was each chip going behind the screen. How many altogether? Stacy answered correctly. Then the interviewer presented Stacy with four and five chips in the same manner. Again, she answered correctly. How did she do it? Previously she had denied counting on fingers.

Probably the denial was the result of her teacher's strong opposition to such methods. Now, however, Stacy admitted to solving the problem by counting. She was able to do 6 + 5 (after an initial error); 10 + 4; 14 + 6. She seemed to count on her fingers, sometimes starting from 1, and sometimes counting on from the larger number. Apparently, Stacy could solve problems involving absent objects, at least when she had the opportunity to see them, however fleetingly, before they were hidden.

These episodes bring out the following points.

1. Even children who fail badly seem to possess some kind of intellectual strengths that can be used as a basis for learning. At the outset, Stacy's behavior seemed chaotic; she appeared to be retarded. Everything she did confirmed the teacher's judgment that she had the most difficulty of anyone in the class. She could not do anything right, and we felt quite hopeless about helping her. Nevertheless, subsequent interviewing showed that she had some basic skills, especially for dealing with concrete objects. I believe that if you dig deep enough you will find in virtually all children a core of arithmetic skills on which they can build. At least that has been our experience with every child we have seen.

2. The child's hidden strengths usually involve some form of counting. Stacy could add by counting sets or by counting on from the larger number. We have seen repeatedly that children frequently use some variant of counting in their arithmetic work. Do we stress counting enough in our curricula?

3. Intellectual success helps to alleviate emotional difficulties. At the outset, it was abundantly clear that Stacy was depressed. She was lethargic, she seemed miserable, it was hard to get her to say anything. All this was typical of her ordinary classroom behavior. We do not know the reason for her depression: perhaps it was linked to some events at home; perhaps it was the result of her failure to learn in school; or perhaps it stemmed from some combination of the two. Whatever its causes, her depression seems to have been alleviated by her improved performance in arithmetic. When the interviewer succeeded in discovering some of Stacy's competencies and in getting her to use them, her entire manner changed: she seemed more alert, more lively, she had some sparkle. Stacy seemed to enjoy seeing herself as a child with ability. Children's self-concept is usually bound up with their intellectual achievements. In some cases, helping children to improve their schoolwork may do more for their emotional health than well-meaning attempts to analyze and treat their emotional disturbances directly.

4. Informal methods often play a key role in getting to know and in helping children with problems. On discovering how badly Stacy did on ordinary arithmetic problems, the interviewer introduced concrete tasks, phrased them in ways that Stacy could understand, and attempted, in a deliberately nonstandardized way, to tailor the testing of her strengths. This procedure seemed to relax her, to reduce her anxieties about being tested, and provided her with opportunities to show and discover what she could do. The interview also suggested some very specific ways of helping her—for example, by developing her finger counting.

By contrast, standard tests are of little value in a case like Stacy's. They often frighten children doing badly. They yield unhelpful labels like "low mathematical aptitude". And worst of all, they fail to reveal children's strengths. The tests say nothing specific about what the child can do and about how instruction should proceed. All this is positively harmful to the child who has trouble learning.

Understanding

In the last two chapters we have examined mistakes, their origins, and gaps in children's thinking; we have studied four children with severe difficulties in school arithmetic. Now we shall change the focus and consider *real understanding*. (We already touched on this in Chapter 5, when we considered the understanding of written numbers.) This seems to take two major forms. One is *perceiving* accurately and the other is *making connections* among various areas of knowledge, including one's intuition.

CONNECTING

Many children calculate quite accurately, but without genuine understanding. Correct answers may indicate only a mechanical approach.

At 9–5, Deborah did a simple addition problem on paper, 13 + 15. She described with precision how to do the calculation. Add the 3 and the 5, then the 1 and the 1. But what about her understanding of the process?

I: What do the two 1's stand for?

D: 2.

I. But there's no "two," there's 28.

D: There's two 1's here and you add them up.

I: But what do these 1's stand for?

D: What do you mean? For 13 and 15.

I: One stands for 13?

D: I don't understand what you mean.

Obviously, Deborah did not understand column addition; she could merely do it.

Similarly, Alice added 20 + 4 on paper and got the correct result.

I: How come you put the 4 here? Maybe we can put the 4 here and get a whole different answer.

The interviewer wrote:

$$
\begin{array}{r}
20 \\
+\ 4 \\
\hline
\end{array}
$$

A: We can't do that.

I: Why not?

A: You just couldn't do that.

I: Any reason?

A: You just can't.

I: Here, I'm going to do it. You said I can't, but I'm going to do it.

A: But you can't. It won't be the right answer.

We have seen examples like these before. They serve to remind us that many children simply calculate without understanding much if anything of the underlying rationale. Such mechanical calculation seems quite common and for many individuals may even persist throughout life. But some children come to understand calculation: they make a *connection* between the calculational routines taught in school and various aspects of their knowledge. It is to this process of connecting—gaining insight or meaning through the integration of various areas of knowledge—that we now turn.

Connecting with something simpler

One way to understand a written calculation or algorithm is to interpret it in terms of a simpler procedure. Children often *assimilate* (Piaget's concept again) the codified procedures taught in school into their more elementary and comfortable counting schemes.

A very simple example of this was given by Sonya, a first grader, who was asked why she wrote 6 + 3 = 9 on paper.

S: This is 6 + 3 = 9 and I put a 9 here, just remembering. Some people

say 6 + 3 is 8: they get their answers wrong. But 6 + 3 is 9 'cause you
can tell . . . adding 3 more is 9 . . . 6, 7, 8, 9. [She counted on her
fingers.]

Sonya understood a conventional arithmetic fact—6 + 3 = 9—
in terms of her own counting. She accepted the written formula because she could get the same results by counting on her fingers. In a
sense, her counting understood her writing.

Later Sonya was asked to add eight imaginary dots and four
imaginary dots. To do this she used a mental procedure: she mistakenly remembered that 8 + 3 = 10 and then added one more to get
11 as the answer. The interviewer asked her to check the answer.
Sonya wrote 8 + 4 = . Then she placed eight dots around the 8 and
four dots around the 4. She then counted the dots, saying, "So 8 and
4 is 1, 2, 3, 4, 5, 6, 7, 8. Now this is 8, 9, 10, then 11. No, it's 12."

For Sonya, written symbolism—the 8 + 4 = —made sense only
insofar as she could connect it with counting. She understood the
written formula only in terms of the counting of dots.

The child may also understand multiplication in terms of counting. Kathy was asked to compare 6 + 6 with 6 × 6.

I: Which one do you think will give you the biggest number for the
answer?

K: Times.

I: Why?

K: Well, 6 × 6 is more than 6 + 6 'cause you have to count six times
instead of only two times.

Kathy assimilated both addition and multiplication into counting by sixes. To get 6 + 6, you count by sixes two times. To get
6 × 6, you count by sixes six times. By interpreting written calculations in terms of a simpler, common language—counting by sixes—
Kathy was able to make the requested comparison.

At 9–5, on the same day as she was unable to explain place
value in column addition, Deborah was asked to do a problem in division. She wrote 9)1,234 and said out loud as she calculated,
"How many groups of 9 are there in 1,234? That's the problem. How
much does 9 go into 1? Zero times, so you can't do it. So it's impossible and you write a zero. Then you ask how many times does 9
go into 12. And it goes in one time and there is some leftovers. 10,
11, 12—there are three leftovers. Now, how much does 9 go into
33? . . ."

For the most part, Deborah's solution was quite straightforward.

She used the standard division algorithm, supplemented by some counting. For example, to subtract 9 from 12, she used counting to get the "leftovers." What interested the interviewer was Deborah's opening remark, "How many groups of 9 are there in 1,234?" The interviewer thought that this was simply an empty verbalism. Deborah was merely parroting a meaningless phrase picked up in school.

I: Very good. You said at the beginning, "How many groups of 9 are there in 1,234?" What do you mean, how many "groups" of 9?

D: If you want to do it this different way, you can count in the nine tables until you get up to 1,234.

I: How would you do that, just start?

D: I would go: 9, 18, 27, 36, 45, 54, 63, 72, 81, 90, and whatever comes after that.

I: What does that mean?

D: You count nines tables until you got up to 1,234.

I: And what would that tell you?

D: You'd see how many nines there were.

So Deborah really had understood the notion "groups of 9." She gave meaning to the concept by assimilating it into repeated counting by nines. This resulted in an excellent explanation. The interviewer's initial impression that "groups of 9" represented only an empty verbalization was clearly incorrect.

Deborah's behavior offers another example of children's inconsistency: she seemed to understand groups but not the role of place value in addition.

Connecting with formal knowledge

While some children interpret a calculation in terms of counting, others understand calculation in terms of formal mathematical theory. They assimilate calculational routines into other aspects of their formal mathematical knowledge.

At 9–9, Rebecca was struggling with the connection between the mechanics of borrowing and place value theory. Rebecca had done:

$$
\begin{array}{r}
{}^{7}\!\!\not{8}\;\;{}^{13}\!\not{4}\;\;{}^{1}6 \\
-\;6\;\;\;6\;\;7 \\
\hline
1\;\;\;7\;\;9
\end{array}
$$

by the standard borrowing technique.

I: Now what are you doing when you cross out the 4 and make a 3? What does that mean?

R: Borrowing.

I: What are you borrowing? You took a 1 from the 4 and put it next to the six. What is that 1? How come you can take 1 from the 4?

R: 'Cause you crossed out the 4 and made it a 3.

I: What is the 1? Is it one thing or what?

R: It comes from the tens.

I: You took one 10 from the tens? How come you get 16?

R: 10 + 6 make 16.

The examiner then asked about the 1 written above the 4, with the 3.

I: What's the 1? Is that a 10?

R: No, it's hundreds.

I: So what's this number here? The 13 is really what?

R: 103.

I: 103? Are you sure? The 3 is, is it ones or tens?

R: The 3 is from the tens. 130.

I: So 130 minus what?

R: Minus 6.

I: Does that really mean 6?

R: It could mean 16.

I: 60?

R: 60, I mean . . . Oh, I get it now. But that's not how I do it in school.

We see that Rebecca was beginning to see how borrowing works in terms of place value. She saw that the one borrowed from the second column was *really* a ten, and the one borrowed from the leftmost column was *really* a hundred. She could see this only because she understood something about place value theory. She was making some sense of calculation because she could connect it with her abstract knowledge of mathematics.

Jane, whose work we have already reviewed in Chapter 6, exhibits a similar kind of process. She was doing a subtraction problem and tried to check it by doing addition. She wrote:

$$\begin{array}{r} \overset{1}{9}3899 \\ + 913 \\ \hline 185199 \end{array}$$

The interviewer told Jane that this was the wrong answer, but did not instruct her in how to do the calculation properly. He gave her a new problem, namely subtract 14 from 132. At first Jane wrote:

$$
\begin{array}{r}
132 \\
-\ 14 \\
\hline
\end{array}
$$

Jane looked puzzled. She said, "Maybe it's supposed to go like this":

$$
\begin{array}{r}
132 \\
-\ 14 \\
\hline
\end{array}
$$

Jane looked perplexed. She said, "Maybe . . . no . . . yes!"

At this point, Jane had a look of real insight and excitement. "That's the way it's supposed to go, because that's in the ones place, that's in the tens place and that's in the hundreds place." As she said this, she pointed to the appropriate numerals in both 132 and 14. She then proceeded to solve the problem.

This shows how understanding can improve performance. At first, Jane used a faulty algorithm—she lined up numbers from left to right. She saw how to correct her mistake only when she understood the algorithm by connecting it with her knowledge of place value. This allowed Jane to see exactly where she had gone wrong and to improve her calculations.

A few children exhibit a surprisingly harmonious integration between their calculational routines and formal theory.

Kathy did $6 \times 12 = 72$.

K: Six times two is twelve. I put down the 2 and carried the 1.

I: What does that mean to carry the 1?

K: Well, it's 10. You can't put 12 in the ones column, 'cause 12 just happens to have a ten in it. For each 10, you just leave how many ones you have there and you carry the 1.

I: How did you get the 7?

K: 'Cause I added this [1 + 6].

I: But you said it was one 10.

K: These are all tens [meaning 6 + 1 is really 60 + 10] so it's 70.

Kathy seemed to know at each step how to interpret the multiplication algorithm in terms of place value.

Connecting with informal knowledge

We have seen how children try to understand the written procedures taught in school by connecting them with counting schemes or with formal knowledge. Now we consider yet another form of connecting: relating written procedures to informal knowledge. Here children understand by trusting their intuition, by relying on their common sense.

Jennifer, a third grader, eight years of age, was working on problems of long division and experiencing a certain amount of difficulty.[1] She was presented with the problem of dividing 8 into 4,808. Jennifer's teacher asked her to indicate how she went about solving a problem of this sort. Jennifer said that "8 doesn't go into 4, so you have to say that 8 goes into 48, six times." She wrote:

$$\begin{array}{r} 6 \\ 8{\overline{\smash{)}\,4{,}808}} \end{array}$$

So far Jennifer was employing the usual long division method.

I: All right. What do you do next?

J: The zero doesn't count for anything, so you say, "8 goes into 8 once."

She wrote:

$$\begin{array}{r} 6\ \ 1 \\ 8{\overline{\smash{)}\,4{,}808}} \end{array}$$

We see then that to do division Jennifer employed a rather unique calculational procedure. She systematically omitted the zero, and did so because she explicitly believed that "the zero doesn't count for anything."

Next, the interviewer wanted to see how seriously Jennifer believed in this mistaken bit of formal knowledge.

I: Would these two problems be the same?

The interviewer wrote:

$$8{\overline{\smash{)}\,488}} \qquad 8{\overline{\smash{)}\,4{,}808}}$$

J: Yes.

Jennifer calculated each problem, and in each case obtained the answer 61.

The teacher then asked Jennifer to calculate 800 divided by 8. Jennifer said, "8 goes into 8 once."

$$\frac{1}{8)\overline{800}}$$

Given Jennifer's rule, it was entirely plausible for her to get an answer of 1. Next the teacher asked Jennifer: "Which of these is the largest?"

$$8 \qquad\qquad 80 \qquad\qquad 800$$

Jennifer replied, "They are all the same. Zero doesn't make any difference."

We can interpret Jennifer's behavior to this point as follows. First, she had a very odd algorithm for dividing: she systematically ignored zero, with the result that she considered $8)\overline{8}$ the same as $8)\overline{80}$. She even ignored zero in comparing the magnitude of numbers so that 8 was seen to equal 80. Second, these calculational procedures resulted from her faulty formal knowledge. Her calculation was bad because of its connection with a faulty mathematical theory, namely that "zero makes no difference." Thus, Jennifer's calculation routine and her formal knowledge was integrated: there was no gap between the two. Yet this integration resulted in calculational error because the formal knowledge was wrong. By contrast, Jane's narrowing of the gap between calculation and formal knowledge improved her calculation precisely because her formal knowledge was accurate.

But that is not the end of Jennifer's story. Next the teacher proceeded to explore Jennifer's informal knowledge.

I: How old are you?

J: Eight.

I: Do you have any older brothers or sisters?

J: A brother nine years old and a sister eleven years old.

I: Do you have any friends who are older than your brother but younger than your sister?

J: Oh, somebody who is ten.

I: Can you write ten?

Jennifer wrote 10.

I: Which is larger [she wrote 1 and 10 on paper], 1 or 10?

J: They're both the same because zero doesn't make any difference.

Suddenly an expression of comprehension lit up her face.

J: Oh, that's 1 and that's 10!

We can interpret this example as follows. At the outset, the interviewer had established two things about Jennifer:

1. In calculation, she systematically omitted zero.

2. She believed on a very explicit level that zero makes no difference.

Now the examiner had added a third bit of information:

3. Her informal knowledge of ages involved an accurate ordering of numbers by magnitude.

We have already seen that, out of school, children acquire considerable informal knowledge concerning money, relations among ages, and so on. Jennifer displayed a good working knowledge of ages. As a result of ordinary experience in the world, she knew that nine years is younger than ten years and that eleven years is older than ten years. No doubt she also believed that a one-year-old is younger than a ten-year-old. She could order ages in terms of relative magnitude.

Jennifer's informal knowledge of ages existed separately from her knowledge of written mathematics. As in so many other children, there was a gap between her informal and formal knowledge. She normally heard ages spoken, not written on paper. While she believed that "ten" is greater than "one," she did not know that 10 is greater than 1, and that therefore zero does make a difference.

So Jennifer's knowledge was complex. Her knowledge of ages told her that "one" is smaller than "ten." At the same time, her calculations told her that 1 = 10; and her mathematical theory held that zero doesn't make any difference.

During the course of the interview, Jennifer was led to make a connection—to narrow the gap—between her informal knowledge and the other systems. She already knew that someone who is "ten" years old is older than someone who is "one" year old. Then, in the interview, she saw a 1 and 10 on paper and, applying her rule that zero doesn't make any difference, concluded that 1 is the same as 10. But then she perceived the inconsistency between that conclusion and her knowledge that "one" is less than "ten" when years are involved. Given this inconsistency, Jennifer decided that her informal knowledge was sounder than her mathematical theory. She then connected the written numbers 1 and 10 with her informal knowledge. She said, "Oh, that's *one*, and that's *ten!*" This expressed the insight that the 1 on paper was very much like the "one" year; and that the 10 on paper was very much like the "ten" in years. She concluded that the two written numerals were therefore not the same. Jennifer drew on her informal knowledge of years to attribute meaning to the written numerals. She trusted her intuitions more than her mathematical theory.

After the insight concerning 1 and 10, Jennifer decided to redo some of the problems that she had failed earlier. She saw that 8 < 80 < 800; and she tried long division again, eventually achieving some degree of success.

SUMMARY

Obviously, many children fail to understand the calculations that they perform correctly. Other children understand by making connections between the calculations and other aspects of their knowledge. One type of connection involves a link between a written calculation and a simpler procedure like counting on the fingers. Children *assimilate* difficult material into more elementary schemes. Another type of connection involves formal knowledge: children comprehend a calculation in terms of abstract mathematical principles. Thus, they may interpret column addition in terms of place value theory. A third connection is with informal knowledge. Children trust their intuition; they understand mathematics in common-sense terms. For years they have been building up a body of informal mathematical knowledge. Now they use it to give meaning to written calculations.

PRINCIPLES

1. *There are different kinds of understanding.* Some children understand written number as counting, others as ages, and still others in terms of mathematical principles. The written 4 is like "one, two, three, four" on the fingers; or like four-years-old; or it is a union of sets. Children differ in their approaches, and each approach has some validity. Four-on-the-fingers offers a link to expert count-

ing routines; four-years-old connects with a solid body of informal knowledge; four-as-sets leads into mathematical theory. Perhaps all forms of understanding should be encouraged.

2. *Understanding often requires a connection with the specific.* For many, if not all children, learning and understanding must originate in contact with specific instances and concrete things. Children must count on their fingers, or compare numbers with ages, or calculate problems over and over again. Only then does written mathematics acquire meaning. Moreover, it may even be true that children can understand abstract mathematical principles only after they have had specific and concrete experience. The recitation of mathematical theory does not in itself produce understanding.

PERCEIVING

Children must learn not only to calculate, but to *perceive*, to *see*. They must learn that mathematics is concerned with important regularities, and that numbers behave in orderly ways that they can predict.

Consider first a child who fails to see a very simple regularity. Barbara, six years of age, an English girl, was learning simple addition with some blocks of different lengths, each divided into units of constant size. If asked to find the sum of 4 and 2, she would combine a 4-block with a 2-block, count the total number of subdivisions on the blocks, and thus achieve the solution (see Figure 8–1). After she did this a while, the interviewer gave her the following problems, written on paper as the teacher would ordinarily do, one after the other:

$$\begin{array}{cccccccc} 5 & 7 & 3 & 2 & 4 & 3 & 5 & 3 \\ +7 & +5 & +2 & +3 & +3 & +4 & +3 & +5 \end{array}$$

In every case, she used the blocks to achieve a solution. She simply combined two appropriate blocks and counted the total number of subdivisions. First, she did 5 combined with 7 and then 7 combined with 5. She always got the correct answer (or a slightly incorrect answer because of counting errors).

So Barbara used a sensible strategy—combining and counting—to calculate accurately. Her behavior was correct; she made the right responses. Yet the correctness of her solutions is only a minor and misleading part of her behavior. More important is the fact that she

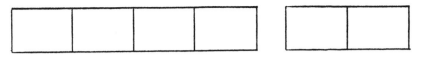

Figure 8–1. *Barbara's addition*

did not understand the problem. She failed to see a very important regularity in the numbers: the order of addition does not change the result. This principle of commutativity states that 5 + 7 gives you the same answer as 7 + 5. The evidence for commutativity was abundant: the problems on the paper showed that 5 + 7 = 12 and 7 + 5 = 12; 3 + 2 = 5 and 2 + 3 = 5; 4 + 3 = 7 and 3 + 4 = 7. Yet Barbara did not perceive the underlying rule, that order makes no difference. The evidence was there for her to see, but she did not take advantage of it.

Barbara's failure to perceive commutativity then affected her behavior. She had to solve each problem separately. Having done 4 + 3, she then had to do 3 + 4 all over again. Had she seen the principle, she could have short-cut the laborious process of calculation and gotten the same, correct answers in a much easier way. Perceiving underlying rules can lead to economy and efficiency; failing to perceive can result in rigidity and inflexibility.

We can only speculate on the reasons for Barbara's failure to see commutativity. On the one hand, perhaps her attention was narrowly focussed and restricted to the operations necessary to solve each problem. She may have been so wrapped up in solving 5 + 7 and 7 + 5 as individual problems that she did not even see that the same numbers were involved in both cases. She then could not compare the results for different problems. Her narrow attention may therefore have resulted in a failure to obtain knowledge concerning commutativity. On the other hand, Barbara's difficulty may have resulted not from a narrowly focussed attention, but from a failure to appreciate what she was attending to. That is, perhaps Barbara did see that the same numbers were involved in the various problems, but nevertheless failed to appreciate the significance of this fact. Whichever of the possibilities is correct, Barbara did not perceive commutativity, and this resulted in ineffective computation.

Let us summarize the important aspects of the observation on Barbara's addition. (1) She could calculate accurately, coming up with the right answers, but did not understand. (2) Her lack of understanding consisted of a failure to perceive an important regularity in arithmetic. (3) The evidence for the regularity was abundant, but Barbara failed either to consider the evidence or to appreciate its implications. (4) This resulted in rigid, inflexible calculation.

The situation is analogous to what we have already seen in the case of young children learning to count. They encounter the world of numbers when they hear their parents say, "one, two, three. . . ." This is analogous to Barbara's experience with addition problems. Young children soon see that underlying the counting numbers there is a deeper reality—a set of rules. They perceive the principles that allow them to construct "fifty-one, fifty-*two*. . . ." or "one million, three hundred, and fifty-one, fifty-*two*. . . ." This is analogous to the commutativity rule that Barbara could have discovered. If young children did not learn to perceive the rules, they would have to memorize the sequence of counting numbers, and this would be even more awkward than Barbara's repetitious calculations.

So in both counting and addition there is a world of numbers that in a sense exist apart from the child. These behave in regular ways and give clues to underlying principles or structure. To understand the numbers, the child needs to perceive the deeper reality.

Several observations show that children learn to perceive regularities like commutativity in several steps. For example, Diana, a third grader, believed quite firmly that 20 + 14 is the same as 14 + 20. "Twenty and 14 is the same question . . . that's the same thing. . . . All you do is put that number backwards."

I: Do you think it always works with other numbers?

D: Yeah. Except for times.

So Diana did not yet perceive that commutativity holds for multiplication as well as addition.

Similarly Ronnie, a second grader, believed in commutativity for small numbers but was unsure about larger ones.

I: How much is 3 + 2?

R: 5.

I: How much is 2 + 3?

R: 5.

I: How come it's the same?

R: I dunno. It just is.

I: Just is. Do you think it'll always be like that if I just turned the numbers around?

R: Yeah, no matter how many times you turn around.

Perceiving reality in language

The same sort of thing happens when children learn to talk. They are immersed in the world of language when they hear people speak. This provides them with abundant evidence from which they must abstract the underlying rules of language. From hearing "walked" and "talked" and the like, they must perceive a rule for constructing the past tense. The perception of such rules is required for efficient speaking. It is easier to remember a rule for the past tense than to remember the past tense of each verb separately.

Hearing speech is like seeing sums on paper. Abstracting the rules for the past tense is like perceiving commutativity. Speaking by rule is like short-cutting calculation.

Yet when Ronnie was given $3 + 9$ and $9 + 3$, he felt that he had to count up the sum each time. Perhaps he had had less experience with larger numbers and consequently was not yet sure that commutativity holds for them too.

Some children are very cautious in their generalizations concerning commutativity. Thus, Chris, a second grader, recognized that $8 + 4$ is the same as $4 + 8$, when collections of dots are involved.

I: How do you know that?

C: Because it's the same.

I: It's not the same. It's switched around. So how's it the same?

C: It has to be. Because 8 and 4 are 12. 4 and 8 are 12 too.

I: Do you think it would work with any dots in the first box and any in the second all the time?

C: I'm not sure.

As perceptual learning progresses, children learn that commutativity holds in some contexts but not in others. Lori, a third grader, maintained that $20 + 14$ yields the same result as $14 + 20$ because "it's the other way around."

I: Just because it's the other way around it's the same thing?

L: Yeah, unless it's minus or something.

These observations provide insight into how children learn to see regularities in numbers. A prerequisite seems to be that children have experience in calculating a great many arithmetic problems. They must be immersed in the world of numbers. Over the years, they work $6 + 7$, $7 + 6$, 7×6, 7×6, 6×7, $7 \div 6$, $6 \div 7$. At first, the very act of calculation may be so difficult that they focus attention only on individual problems. They concentrate on getting the correct sum for say $6 + 7$ and so they cannot notice that $7 + 6$ yields the same result. Or it is so hard for them to do $7 \div 6$ that they cannot see that $6 \div 7$ gives a different answer.

After a period of time, however, the process of calculation becomes easier and more accurate so that children need not concentrate so much effort on it. Now it is possible for them to direct their attention to relations among problems. They can now perceive various regularities—that $6 + 7 = 7 + 6$ and $6 \times 7 = 7 \times 6$. They see the absence of other regularities—that $6 \div 7 \neq 7 \div 6$ and that $7 \times 6 \neq 6 - 7$. They learn that the pattern holds for addition and multiplication but not for subtraction and division. They learn too that commutativity holds for the relatively large numbers that they have had little contact with as well as for the relatively small numbers they have worked with frequently. In this way do children gradually learn the nature and limits of commutativity.

Several cautions: one is that not all children manage to learn all this. Many children do not learn to perceive the structure underlying numbers and therefore continue to calculate in a blind, although often correct, fashion. Second, many children *talk* as if they appreciate certain regularities but really do not; they are merely parroting an empty verbalization learned in school. Thus, Alice, a third grader, maintained that commutativity does not work for subtraction. In support of this she offered, in a singsong voice, a verbal formula: " 'Cause the first number in take away has to be more." This apparently meant that in subtraction you cannot have a statement like 6×7, and so the problem of commutativity does not arise. The interviewer asked, "Are you sure?" Alice answered vehemently, "Yes, I'm sure. My teacher says it all the time."

Third, learning about patterns like commutativity depends on accurate calculation. An example makes this clear.[2] Joe was presented with three addition problems, all involving the same numbers, and solved them as follows:

379	427	16
16	379	427
+ 427	+ 16	+ 379
922	812	822

I: If you have the same numbers, are your answers going to be the same?

J: No. Because they are switched around and one number is harder than another sometimes.

I: What happens to the answer?

J: It might get bigger or smaller.

Joe apparently meant that it was harder for him to add up the numbers in some sequences than others. Perhaps Joe found some addition facts harder to remember than others. In any event, when he added the same numbers he got three different answers. The numbers that Joe works with are not well-behaved—they fail to show that order makes no difference. And if Joe accurately perceived the behavior of *his* numbers, he must conclude that commutativity is not a fact of mathematical life.

Obviously, to perceive valid mathematical principles, Joe needs experience with well-behaved numbers. He needs the opportunity to perceive valid patterns in numbers. Since he cannot create such patterns himself, someone else will have to do it. In a sense, Joe needs to *do* less so that he can see more.

Children also learn about other, more complex regularities. Here is a case of perceiving a pattern in the case of division. Peter, thirteen years of age, was given two division problems, namely $10\overline{)150}$ and $10\overline{)1,500}$ and did them correctly.

I: Take a look at these. You've done these two. 10 into 150 was 15, and 10 into 1,500 was 150. Can you guess what this one is going to be just by looking at those two?

The interviewer wrote $10\overline{)15,000}$.

I: Anything that helps you there [he pointed at the two previous problems]?

Peter did not answer. He just wrote 1,500 in the quotients' place.

I: 1,500. How did you get that?

P: This 15 here is like the other 15 there. Just add another zero.

Later he did $10\overline{)2,300}$ correctly and apparently in the same way. There was a pattern in the previous problems that Peter had solved, and Peter saw the pattern. He did not need to be told or rewarded: experience with the numbers somehow allowed him to see the pattern. At the same time, his perception was probably very primitive. Most likely all he saw was that as a zero was added to the dividend, so a zero was added to the quotient. Undoubtedly, Peter could not explain this in any way, for example, in terms of powers of ten.

Here is a more complex example of perceiving a pattern—this time a function.

A 7–4, Alexandria was with her family as they were getting out of the automobile and entering the house.³ Alexandria spontaneously volunteered, "When Paul is eighteen, I will be twenty." Paul was her brother, then five years of age.

Her father said; "My word, how did you figure that out?"

Alexandria said; "See, it's easy. You just go: 5, 6, 7; or 8, 9, 10 so it's 18, 19, 20. So when Paul is eighteen I'll be twenty." In saying the preceding numbers, Alexandria placed a heavy rhythmic stress on the middle word in each triplet.

Alexandria had perceived that her age is always two more than her brother's. While obviously unable to state it in explicit form, she had uncovered a functional relation of the form $x + 2 = y$, where x is her brother's age and y is hers. Moreover, she used counting as a method for calculating the function: thus, 8, 9, 10 or 18, 19, 20.

This sort of thing is not uncommon. Children frequently encounter different ages and are concerned to establish the relations among them. Children want to know who is older than whom and by how much, since age is tied up with status.

Here is another example. At age four, Chris spontaneously began to compare his age with Jay's, his brother's.⁴

C: After I'm four, I'll be five.

I: How old will you be after you'll be five?

C: Six. And Jay'll be seven.

I: When you're six, Jay will be seven.

C: Yep. And then I'll be seven and Jay'll be eight. Oh, Jay'll be ahead of me.

I: Where will Jay be ahead of you?

C: In growing up.

I: I see. After you're seven and Jay's eight, how old will you be?

C: Eight.

I: And how old will Jay be?

C: I really don't know the number after 8.

Chris had seen a function: Jay is always one year older than he. Like Alexandria, Chris computed the function simply by counting on.*

Sometimes children's perception of regularities is most impressive. Court provides a fascinating example concerning her son Paul.

Once when he was 7 years 7 months old, his father showed him that 12345679 × 9 gives 111111111. Then after Paul verified this and showed it to others with glee, his father told him the next evening to multiply 12345679 by 18. The answer was 222222222. When, after having performed the multiplication Paul came to his father with the answer, he said: "Next I guess you will make me multiply the same number by 27." "Why," asked his father, taken aback, "and what would come of it if I did?" "I would get all threes, I guess; and by 36 will come out all fours."[5]

Paul had seen this pattern. If 9 × 12345679 = 111111111, then 2(9) × 12345679 = 2(111111111) and 3(9) × 12345679 = 3 (111111111). He had seen what a constant does. In general terms, if a × b = c, then n (a) × b = n (c).

Kris provides another example of perceiving complex patterns.[6] The interviewer asked her to do 9 × 8 and she immediately responded 72, apparently by remembering the relevant product. Asked to figure out the product, she wrote 8 + 8 + 8 + 8 + 8 + 8 + 8 + 8 + 8 = 72 and 9 + 9 + 9 + 9 + 9 + 9 + 9 + 9 = 72. She also did the problem in the form × 8. First, she wrote

$$\begin{array}{r} 9 \\ \times\,8 \\ \hline 7 \end{array}$$

and as she did so remarked that "one less than 8 is 7." In other words, the first digit of the answer seemed to be one less than the multiplier. She then tried to figure out what rule might result in the next number, the 2 in 72. She wrote:

$$9 \times 6 = 54$$
$$9 \times 7 = 63$$
$$9 \times 8 = 72$$

She saw that in each case, the first digit of the product is one less than the multiplier. Thus, in 9 × 6 = 54, the 5 in 54 is one less

*The perception of functions by a four-year-old should not surprise us. Remember the infant's perception of functions in Chapter 2.

than the multiplier 6. Also, there seemed to be a rule that could give the second digit of the product. For $\begin{array}{r}9\\\times\,8\\\hline 7\end{array}$, the rule could be stated "7 and what makes 9? 2. That's the missing number." In other words, if you have a problem like $\begin{array}{r}9\\\times\,5\\\hline 4\end{array}$ (where you already know that the first number of the product is 4 since $5 - 1 = 4$), you simply subtract the first number of the product from the 9 to get the second number in the product.

Now this is an unusual rule, and perhaps Kris was the first person to have discovered this particular set of regularities in multiplication.* But the rule itself is not crucial. More important is the fact that "this certainly was a very creative, human activity, using basic mathematics skill."[7]

SUMMARY

One aspect of understanding is *perceiving*. Children must learn to see the regularities that underlie the behavior of numbers. At first, they fail to do this. For example, in addition they laboriously calculate each problem separately. Having done $2 + 1 = 3$, they do not know that $1 + 2$ gives the same answer because they have failed to perceive the simple rule that order makes no difference in adding. Ignorance of the rule results in rigid and inflexible calculation. The process of perceptual learning—learning to perceive the rules—occurs over a long period of time and in several steps. For example, children may first discover commutativity for addition and only later for multiplication, or they may perceive commutativity for small numbers, but not larger ones. As time goes on, children can discover genuinely interesting and complex rules that can be of considerable aid in calculation.

PRINCIPLE

A crucial aspect of learning mathematics is learning to perceive. Children need to learn not only how to execute calculations. They must learn to see how numbers behave, and to detect underlying patterns and regularities. This aspect of mathematics education—accurate perception—does not receive sufficient attention.

---

*Try to generalize the rule to other cases of multiplication. It works, after some slight modification.

Chapter 9

Testing and Teaching

This chapter discusses helping school children to learn arithmetic. The psychological knowledge discussed in this book—childrens understanding of symbolism, their invented strategies, the gaps between their formal and informal knowledge—can provide teacher and parent with useful ideas for conducting education in mathematics. Knowledge of children's arithmetic can help you to test children and to teach them. It can help you to understand the individual child and to alleviate problems of learning and understanding. It may even provide certain guidelines for curriculum.

While psychological knowledge can make enormous contributions, we must recognize its limits. One is that it cannot provide the teacher with a detailed lesson plan or curriculum for instruction in addition. It cannot give the parent foolproof solutions to children's difficulties. To quote William James again, "You make a great, a very great mistake, if you think that psychology, being the science of the mind's laws, is something from which you can deduce definite programmes and schemes and methods of instruction for immediate schoolroom use." There is no mechanical formula—no cookbook—based on psychology or anything else, guaranteed to produce success in the teaching of mathematics.

A second limit is that sensitivity is required to apply psychological principles to the individual case. Good ideas can easily be misused. The ideas discussed in this book can provide insight only if they are applied with intelligence and only if an effort is made to attune them to the individual nuance. As James said, "An intermediary inventive mind must make the application, by using its originality."[1]

Here, then, are some ideas on how to help.

1. Go beyond standard tests

Here is what happened when Rebecca, at 9–10, was given a well known standard test.

First she was shown the following numbers written on paper: 18, 21, 24, ___, ___. The interviewer administered the standard instruction: "The three numbers show a certain relationship. Decide what numbers come next in the pattern and write them on the lines."

R: What do you mean?

I: Decide what numbers come next in the pattern and write them on the lines.

Rebecca wrote: 18, 21, 24. Of course she should have written: 27, 30, 33.

R: Let's go to the harder stuff.

Next Rebecca was shown the following dots and numbers:

	A	B	C
. . . . . .	4 × 6	2 × 12	24 × 1
. . . . . .	6 × 4	12 × 2	1 × 24
. . . . . .			
. . . . . .			

The interviewer gave the standard instruction: "Which multiplications are shown by the arrangement of the dots?"

R: What do you mean?

I: Which multiplications are shown by the arrangement of the dots?

R: I don't understand.

I: Are these dots here 4 × 6 or 2 × 12 or something else?

R: You mean one of them is supposed to be . . . I see. Count this first. [She counted by 4's to get 24.] Twenty-four. So this is it [pointing to 4 × 6] and so is this [2 × 12] and also this one [24 × 1].

I: Which one do you think it is really?

R: What do you mean "really"? They're all it!

The interviewer went on to the third problem.

I: The greatest number shown by using the digits 7, 2, 8 only once each is . . . Now you write it down.

R: What do you mean?

I: What is the biggest number you get by using the digits 2, 7, 8?

R: You mean what's the biggest number here? Eight. Can we go on to something harder?

Why had Rebecca gotten these problems wrong? The interviewer decided to talk informally with Rebecca about the incorrect
answers:

I: This time we're going to talk about the questions to find out how you
did it. This said: "The three numbers show a certain relationship.
Decide what numbers come next in the pattern." You wrote: 18, 21, 24.
Why did you write 18 first?

R: Because it was the lowest number.

I: Let's try something else. Suppose we start out with 14. I want you to
guess what comes next each time. The next one is 18. Now what comes
next? Guess.

R: What do you mean?

I: There's a way you can tell each time what the next number is. The
next number is 22.

R: Wait a minute. Fourteen. [Rebecca began to count silently on her
fingers, very intently and for a long period of time.]

I: What's the next one going to be? Guess.

[She continued to count.]

R: Oh, I see, I think I know. She counted again. Twenty-six. That right?

I: Yes. What's the next one?

R: [Very quickly.] Thirty.

I: Next one?

R: Thirty-four.

I: Next one?

R: Thirty-eight.

I: How did you know?

R: Counted by fours.

I: Okay, let's go on. You said that 4 × 6 and 2 × 12 and 24 × 1 were all
right. See, what they want you to do is choose one of these. It's got to
be either 4 × 6 or 6 × 4; or it's got to be 2 × 12 or 12 × 2; or it's got to
be 24 × 1 or 1 × 24. Which one of these tells you how these dots are
arranged?

R: What do you mean?

I: In other words, if you were telling somebody how to write the dots
down on paper.

R: It would be 4 × 6, of course.

I: Why?

R: Because 1, 2, 3, 4 [she counted the rows] and 1, 2, 3, 4, 5, 6 [she counted the columns] . . . . [Before] I thought you wanted to see which one made 24 and so I said all of them.

I: Okay. Next. On this one you said 8. Why?

R: I thought, which is the biggest number.

I: Suppose you had to write a number using all three of these numbers and you could arrange the numbers in any order you wanted. What's the biggest number you could write?

R: What do you mean?

I: Suppose you had to use these three numbers—the 7, the 2, the 8, and you could put any one first, any one second, and any one third. What's the biggest number you could write?

R: Eight hundred and seventy two.

The moral of all this is very simple. Rebecca misunderstood some of the standard test questions but nevertheless understood the basic concepts and could perform the necessary operations. Standard questioning showed only her wrong answers. Informal questioning revealed her underlying competence.

2. Get to know the individual child in an informal manner.

To help, you need to know the individual child in depth. He is different from other children: he adds by remembering some addition facts and then counting on his fingers; other children add by counting on mentally from the larger number. His own behavior is inconsistent: on some occasions he lines up numbers from left to right and on other occasions from right to left. He does unusual things: he subtracts mentally by regrouping and then counting backwards by tens. He displays a unique constellation of strengths and weaknesses: his mental subtraction can be awesome; his written subtraction is amazingly weak.

The basic premise of this book is that knowing the child is the first step toward helping him. Yet getting this knowledge is not easy. For one thing, standard tests do not help much. They provide only vague characterizations of the child's performance. They show perhaps that he does well or poorly. But usually you already know that and are looking for other information. The tests picture the child as being in the sixtieth percentile of mathematical aptitude or in the twenty-sixth percentile of quantitative thinking. These numbers may be useful for those who have nothing better to do than to fiddle with statistics. But a description of the child that is limited to notions of mathematical aptitude or quantitative thinking is of virtually no use to someone working with him or trying to understand him. As we have seen repeatedly, the child's mathematical thinking is complex. You need to understand his intuitions, his errors, his invented strategies. Standard tests—at least of the type available today in the average school—simply do not help you to see these things. You should not rely on the tests. You need other methods.

I believe that the single most important alternative to standard tests is the informal interview. The adult poses for the child a specific, concrete problem, like column addition with three numbers. The adult carefully observes the child's behavior and asks him to "think out loud" when solving the problem. As the child's behavior unfolds, the adult continually makes attempts to figure out the underlying strategy. Why did the child get 14 as an answer? Perhaps he misremembered the sum of 7 and 6. Or perhaps he counted wrong on his fingers. The second interpretation is probably correct; see how his fingers were moving. The adult tries to check the interpretation; he gives a new problem, he asks some critical questions, he makes closer observations. Always the adult tests out interpretations by means of flexible and *deliberately nonstandardized* questioning. The interviewer treats each child as an individual: perhaps unique questions are needed to uncover the child's special pattern of strengths and weaknesses. If the child produces an unusual response, the interviewer feels free to follow up on it with new questions. Informal interviewing is flexible and responsive to the individual case. For the purpose of gaining insight into the individual child's thought—*your* purpose—informal interviewing makes more sense than standard testing.

Some people tell me that, while sensible, informal interviewing is impractical for two reasons. The first is that parents and teachers cannot do it well, and the second is that there is not enough time for it in the ordinary classroom. I fail to find these objections convincing. For one thing, informal interviewing is not so hard. Many of my students manage to do it quite well after only a minimum of training, which mainly involves reading or seeing some interviews. Indeed, many of the best interviews reported in this book were done by novice students. Probably some teachers and parents will find informal interviewing easy and others hard; some will do well and others poorly. The same is true of psychologists who conduct interviews.

The critic may object that there is considerable room for error, for subjectivity in informal interviewing. This is true. The danger is that the adult can lead the child, can suggest answers, and can misinterpret responses. This happens. But I am convinced that the dangers of standard testing are even greater: mislabelling of children, discrimination against minorities, domination over the entire curriculum, and pollution of the school atmosphere. Surely informal testing cannot fail to do better than standard tests.

But is informal testing practical in the classroom? No and yes. It is impractical if the teacher always conducts the class as a group. Then it is difficult to get to know individual children. But if the teacher runs the class in such a way as to maintain contact with individual students, then informal interviewing is possible.

Not only is it possible, it is both economical and valuable. De Jonghe, who conducted the interview with George (Chapter 7) has the following to report:

> Considering the amount and quality of the information obtained, the informal interview technique is economical both in terms of time and money. Unlike standardized tests, it costs nothing to administer or score. The sheer bulk of information in George's case study may suggest that the technique is impractically time consuming. Yet all this data was collected in a total of two hours. Many standardized tests take that long to administer. When one considers the formidable battery of tests that children are subjected to when referred to a team of learning disabilities specialists as George was, the clinical interview looks parsimonious by comparison. Recently the learning disabilities teacher and I went over my interview data together with the results of the battery of standardized tests which had been administered to him. We found that the test scores confirmed the interview findings while adding little new information except to quantitatively rank George according to grade level against other elementary school students. On the other hand, the interview information often enabled more perceptive interpretation of the test scores. For example, one standardized math test showed George's "mathematical reasoning" ability to be unusually low. When we reviewed the exam questions in this section, we found that they were all number sequence questions. We know that George cannot do number sequences because of his poor counting skills. In other words, his test score on this section does not tell us anything about his supposed mathematical reasoning. Thus the informal interview is both highly effective and economical to use. In addition, it has the advantage that it can be administered by the child's own teacher, and the information applied *directly* to the child's learning environment.[2]

So interviewing can be useful and practical. Try it.

3. Look for the deeper meaning behind children's errors

Children's errors are not capricious. The pattern underlying their mistakes demonstrates that they make them for a reason; they have a meaning that must be discerned. They get wrong answers in addition because they add sideways, line up the numbers incorrectly, or use other faulty strategies. Or they make mistakes because they use an excellent strategy but execute it badly, as when they use mental regrouping to add but misremember a minor addition fact. Errors may have a different meaning for different children, but they always have a meaning.

Having discovered the underlying meaning, you are in a better position to help children. Perhaps their strategy is a slight distortion of a sensible procedure; then you can help them correct the distortion. Perhaps their strategy is sound, but they do not have mastery over the addition facts; then you can help them memorize the facts they need to know. Perhaps the strategy is based on a false mathematical principle, as when Jennifer believed that "zero makes no difference"; then you can correct the principle. There may be as many remedies for errors as there are types of errors. Sometimes the remedy involves the teaching of principles, sometimes drilling by rote. The choice of remedy depends on accurate perception of the error.

In general, it is not useful to think of children's errors in terms of "low IQ," "low mathematical aptitude," perceptual difficulties," or "learning disabilities." Some of these concepts may be fruitfully applied to a very limited number of cases. There do exist some genuine learning disabilities, but they are rare. Similarly, there do exist children who suffer from genuine perceptual problems and from mental retardation. But mental retardation and perceptual dysfunction cannot explain the ordinary child's trouble with mathematics. The jargon provides only the illusion of explanation; in fact, it serves only to obscure ignorance of the real difficulties. Explanations in terms of learning disabilities and perceptual problems are merely a recent fad, hopefully short-lived. Explanations in terms of low IQ or mathematical aptitude have been around a long time, but they are as useless now as they always have been.*

If you are concerned with helping individual children you are not likely to find value in concepts of the kind described above.

---

*The main contribution of the IQ test is exactly what Binet intended it to be: to identify retarded children. This it does reasonably well. But it does not show why they are retarded.

Instead, you need to know the specific roots of mistakes—faulty lining up methods, adding sideways, incorrect memory for the addition facts, and the like. Focus on what you can see, not on abstract psychological ideas like intelligence that have no clear meaning (even to psychologists). It is only when you work at the level of specific detail that you can help.

4. Encourage whatever form of learning seems appropriate for children

Before attempting to help children, it is important to keep in mind a few obvious facts about academic learning. One is that it takes a variety of forms, from the loosely unstructured to the rigidly organized, from the concrete to the abstract. Children learn from drill, from lectures, from reading texts, from observing models, from manipulating real things, from contemplating abstract ideas. Children memorize, listen, observe, imitate, respond, experiment, think. Clearly there are many different learning processes.

Another obvious fact is that each of these processes may be appropriate and effective under various circumstances. Sometimes drill or learning by rote is required, while at other times reading or the manipulation of things is called for. In mathematics, children may need to memorize definitions of terms; they may drill themselves on the use of problem-solving techniques; they read about theorems; they manipulate physical models of mathematical ideas.

It is nonsense to suppose that there is one dominant mode of learning academic material. People have managed to learn, and prefer to learn, under an enormous range of circumstances. Deborah enjoyed using worksheets to help her memorize arithmetic facts. Other children in her class enjoyed playing mathematical games. Still others enjoyed textbooks.

The moral is simple, although the realities of many classrooms make it hard to implement. Explore different kinds of learning for different kinds of children or for the same child under different circumstances. If the child cannot learn by one method, try another. Don't give up on the child; abandon the method. Give some children texts and others games. Do written mathematics with some and informal mathematics with others. If it is necessary to cover a certain text or other body of material with the whole class, then at least supplement this with other approaches for individual children.

Different Kinds of Learning

Halle points out that in the 1830s the Cherokee Indians were 90 percent literate in their native language, despite a lack of schooling. Indeed, it was only *after* the introduction of schooling that the Cherokees developed reading problems. Now, "literacy in Cherokee is attained by many late in life and then almost without benefit of special courses, teachers, or teaching material . . . . A Cherokee will say that it is easy to learn to read Cherokee; . . . one Cherokee claims to have learned to read in an afternoon, stretched out under a tree alone with the Bible."[3] By contrast, Jewish children in Eastern Europe learned to read under highly organized and oppressive conditions. "In Eastern Europe, Jewish children were for generations taught to read and write in Hebrew, a language of which very few had practical command, yet there are no reports that this ever led to the development of massive reading problems. This is especially striking since the teaching methods used in these schools were medieval in their coerciveness and the people to whom teaching was entrusted were, on the whole, held in low esteem by the community."[4]

So reading may be acquired in many ways. It can be learned under a tree or a tyrant.

In brief, we need diversity in teaching. At the same time we should stress methods that allow children to make a connection between their informal knowledge and what is taught in school, as the following principles propose.

5. Show children how school arithmetic relates to their own

Too many children think of school mathematics as an artificial game with no relation to reality. For them, arithmetic is an academic subject—that is, useless, senseless, arbitrary. The aim of the game is to get the right answer, to please the teacher. This is an awful idea for children to have. They must learn instead that school mathematics makes some sense.

Everything we have learned in this book shows that the kind of sense arithmetic can make to a child is not the kind of sense it can make to a mathematician. The arithmetic that is meaningful to a child is the arithmetic of combining objects, of finger counting, of informal notions of "more" and of "take away." This is the arithmetic the child understands and feels comfortable with.

In general, you cannot simply bypass children's arithmetic to teach the mathematician's. To be sure, the mathematician's is in many respects better—it is codified, general, powerful, and perfectly accurate. Despite this, psychological logic dictates that you cater to the weaker ideas of children. Show them how the ideas introduced in school relate to their ways of understanding the world of quantity.

6. Relate written symbolism to what children already know

We have seen that it is extremely difficult for children to understand the written symbolism of mathematics. This is one of their greatest weaknesses in school arithmetic. They may not comprehend a sentence like $7 = 3 + 4$, and they may be unable to write on paper a statement expressing the idea that "four and three is seven." Yet, just as children can speak their native langauge before being able to write it, so they understand a good deal of arithmetic before they can produce its written symbolism. Before his arrival in school, the five or six-year-old already knows something about adding and subtracting and equivalence. Indeed, much of the symbolism children have to learn refers to ideas they already possess in at least a crude form. They know that three dots in horizontal arrangement are the same as three in vertical arrangement, and that you can count them to get "three." All they need to learn is that those arrangements and that "three" can be indicated by 3 on paper. It is not fair to judge children's knowledge of arithmetic from their use of written symbolism. Often children are functionally illiterate with respect to written symbolism but quite adept in informal arithmetic.

To overcome the illiteracy it is necessary to relate the symbolism taught in school to children's already existing knowledge. The introduction of mathematical notation can be frightening—indeed, it may be the first step in mathophobia, the dread of mathematics—if children are not helped to interpret it in terms of familiar ideas. At all stages, arithmetic notation should be connected, as far as possible, to concrete objects and operations on them. The notation for addition can be taught in terms of combining collections of objects; the symbolism for subtraction can be taught in terms of taking away part of a collection from the whole.

A related problem exists with respect to mathematical *language*. Words like *plus, equivalent,* and the like are strange and can easily confuse children. Perhaps the problem can be ameliorated by relating the formal words to children's natural ones, like *take away* and *altogether*. The mathematical words can also be used in the context of concrete objects and manipulations on them.

There is no harm in basing early arithmetic on concrete objects, actions, and informal language. Children will eventually abstract from them more general ideas. Children often reach the general from the particular. In the absence of concrete objects and other specific experiences, children may come to see arithmetic as a kind of arbitrary, meaningless game.

7. Encourage nonstandard means of computation

Children do not always do arithmetic by means of the standard algorithms taught in school. They often use invented strategies based on counting. They add by counting on or by using their fingers. Such methods should be encouraged, not suppressed. Invented strategies are children's own creation; they are comfortable with them and find them meaningful. Also, such methods are often based on sound mathematical principles. Thus, addition can be legitimately interpreted as counting on.

Invented procedures can be used as a vehicle for teaching more abstract mathematical techniques and principles. For example, in Chapter 7, we saw how Bob did addition by regrouping spoken numbers like $22 + 19$ into $(22 + 10) + 9$. This invented procedure could be exploited to teach the ideas of regrouping that lie at the heart of column addition. It is but one step from Bob's procedure $[22 + 19 = (22 + 10) + 9]$ to arrive at the standard algorithm $[22 + 19 = (20 + 10) + (9 + 2)]$ with carrying. The aim of encouraging the child's invented procedures is to improve on them, to make explicit the underlying mathematical principles, and to demonstrate the power and logic of the algorithms. These goals are best achieved through the indirect route of nurturing and extending the child's invented procedures.

8. Exploit unsuspected strengths to reduce the gap between informal and formal knowledge

One of the most significant difficulties in children's arithmetic is the gap between informal and formal knowledge. The phenomenon is widespread: many children have trouble with written work but can cope with the same kind of problem in an informal manner. It is necessary to deal with the gap in several ways.

One is to avoid judging children on the basis of their written work or performance on standard tests, most of which are heavily based on written material. To gain insight into children's real competence, you need to give them the opportunity to try their hand at nonwritten problems, perhaps involving real objects, perhaps stories, perhaps just spoken numbers. Judge them on the ability suggested by their informal mathematics.

A second approach to dealing with the gap is to locate children's unsuspected strengths. It is a remarkable fact that virtually every child we have seen, no matter how poor his performance in school, has demonstrated some kind of basic strength in mathematical thinking. Even Stacy could add and subtract real objects by counting. The first priority then should be given to identifying what the child can do well. Use informal interviewing. Do not be afraid to encourage children's informal mathematics, especially their finger counting.

Third, once the strength is located, try to build on it. Usually it will be an informal skill, like adding by counting on. We have already seen that every effort should be made to relate instruction

Tapping Children's Strengths

Unfortunately, children's strengths often go unrecognized. A few years ago I paid a visit to a well-known clinic that treated children with learning problems. When I asked to see how the psychologist dealt with a typical child, she introduced me to the case of Mark. She told me that Mark had been thoroughly tested. His folder was filled with scores: IQ, readiness, math aptitude, perceptual functioning, and all the rest. I asked what all this showed. The psychologist launched into a dissertation on what was wrong with Mark: all kinds of things. Then I asked what I take to be the obvious question: what can he do well? The psychologist had no idea. It was not a question she had really considered. Later, an informal interview revealed that Mark did not lack informal abilities. The approach of clinical psychology sometimes focuses too strongly on pathology—on weaknesses and problems—rather than on the real strengths that can be used to eliminate the pathology.

generally to informal skills. This approach is even more important when the aim is to correct a severe gap, to reduce the distance between written arithmetic, seen as a meaningless game, and the informal arithmetic which has already proved of some utility.

So exploit the child's strengths. Use Patty's "altogether" to teach her the proper meaning of "plus." Use Bob's regrouping to teach carrying. Use Jennifer's ordering of ages to teach that zero does make a difference. Help children to understand and to enjoy by making a connection between those strange marks on paper and what they already know to be true.

In addition to promoting connections between informal and formal knowledge, there are some other things you can do too.

9. Encourage self-directed learning when you see it

Many children dislike school learning and want to have as little to do with it as possible. This is a fact. But it should not be permitted to obscure an even more important fact: children *can* learn academic material like mathematics or reading "on their own," in a spontaneous and joyous manner. This doesn't happen very often, but it does occur and we have already seen several instances of it. Recall the birthday party at which Deborah and Rebecca invented and enjoyed playing a calculational game in which one child had to add some numbers mentally while another child checked the result on the calculator. Or recall the pizza parlor caper when the children set themselves the task of learning to read bigger and bigger numbers.

Just as children learn on their own to speak, so they *can* learn on their own to do some arithmetic. The difference between the two is this: while *all* children learn in a spontaneous manner to speak, few exhibit the same process with respect to mathematics. In fact, most children prefer not to learn it at all.

The reason for this is unclear. Perhaps the schools are at fault; or, more likely, perhaps academic material cannot usually be learned in a spontaneous fashion. In any event, it is a shame that self-directed learning occurs so infrequently. It can be both effective and enjoyable. And perhaps more importantly, it can teach children certain intellectual habits of "self-government, self-organization, choice."[5] These used to be called virtues, or traits of character. Try to nurture them by trusting the child to learn on his own.

10. Help children to perceive the world of mathematics

One kind of understanding involves the perception of regularities in the behavior of numbers. Children see that order makes no difference in addition but does in subtraction. Or they see that one person's age is greater than another's by a fixed amount. The perception of underlying regularities can have several beneficial effects. It can result in economy and efficiency in problem-solving: by understanding something of the behavior of numbers, children can reduce the tedium of calculation. Accurate perception can also minimize the need for rote learning: seeing that in multiplication the sevens table increases in constant leaps, children need not memorize the table; they can easily construct it (even by counting on their fingers) when they need it. And finally, good perception can lead to the excitement associated with interesting discoveries: it's fun for children to see something new.

Several things can be done to facilitate children's perceptual learning. There already exist various games and curricula that stress the perception of mathematical structure. For example, the Madison Project has developed a functions game in which children are shown results generated by some function, like $x + 3 = y$, and are asked to guess the function. In other words, the children encounter some numbers and must learn to see the rule (the function) that makes them behave as they do. The game is an exercise in perceptual learning.*

Furthermore, the electronic calculator may itself be exploited as a tool for the perception of regularities. The machine can assume much of the burden of calculation. Instead of spending the vast bulk of their time computing, children can have some leisure to observe numbers behave. The calculator can be used to produce well-behaved numbers for examination. Children enjoy pressing the buttons to see what happens. If you repeatedly press the square button, any positive number greater than 1 grows larger and larger at a fantastic (geometric) rate until the calculator overloads. On the other hand, any positive number less than one gets smaller and smaller as you square it and eventually vanishes right off the calculator, which is also fun. Children could not produce by hand all these squares, over and over again, with numbers of any size; they would lose all interest in the problem by the time they laboriously got the data. But

---

*The game is very successful too. I have seen films of culturally deprived students using the game to learn some very interesting and sophisticated mathematics.

the calculator works effortlessly and produces results that are enjoyable to watch and study. In fact, calculators seem to be one of the few mathematical devices that children genuinely enjoy. One children's museum has an exhibit in which children are allowed to play with calculators and it is one of the most popular attractions in the museum.

So relieve children of at least some calculational burdens and encourage them to see what exists in the world of numbers. Use games to do this, and special curricula; and let them use the calculator to produce for themselves well-behaved numbers affording the opportunity for interesting exploration.

CONCLUSION

With these principles in mind—especially a willingness to know children as individuals—you can give a good deal of the help that children need. Perhaps you can meet the challenge of Sonya, who said: "I know how to do two and two. I just gotta learn how to do math."

End Notes

PREFACE

1. James, W. *Talks to teachers on psychology.* New York: Holt, Henry, & Co., 1939. Pp. 7–8.

CHAPTER 1

1. Baldwin, B. T. and Stecher, L. I. *The psychology of the pre-school child.* New York: Appleton, D., & Co., 1925.
2. Drummond, M. *The psychology and teaching of number.* New York: World Book Company, 1922, Page 31.
3. Court, S. R. A. Numbers, time, and space in the first five years of a child's life. *Pedagogical Seminary,* 27 (1920): 71–89.
4. Court, S. R. A. Self-taught arithmetic from the age of five to the age of eight. *Pedagogical Seminary,* 30 (1923): 51–68. Pp. 52–53.
5. Grossman, A. The case of John. Unpublished manuscript. Cornell University, 1976.
6. Drummond, M. *Psychology and teaching of number.* Pp. 25, 32.
7. Court, S. R. A. Self-taught arithmetic. Page 52.
8. Posner, J. K. Personal communication. 1976.
9. Potter, M. C. and Levy, E. J. Spatial enumeration without counting. *Child Development,* 39 (1968): 265–273.
10. Piaget, J. *The child's conception of number.* London: Routledge & Kegan Paul, 1952a.
11. Conant, L. L. Counting. In J. R. Newman (Ed.), *The world of mathematics,* Vol. 1. New York: Simon and Schuster, 1956. Pp 432–441.
12. Baldwin, B. T. and Stecher, L. I. *The psychology of the pre-school child.*
13. Gay, J. and Cole, M. *The new mathematics and an old culture.* New York: Holt, Rinehart and Winston, 1967.

14. Posner, J. K. Personal communication. 1976.
15. Churchill, E. M. *Counting and Measuring.* Toronto: University of Toronto Press, 1961.
16. Riess, A. An analysis of children's number responses. *Harvard Educational Review,* 13 (1943): 149–162.
17. Renwick, E. *Children learning mathematics.* Elms Court, England: Arthur H. Stockwell, 1963.
18. Wertheimer, M. Numbers and numerical concepts in primitive peoples. In W. D. Ellis (Ed.), *A sourcebook of gestalt psychology.* New York:
    Humanities Press, 1967.
19. Zaslavsky, C. *Africa counts.* Boston: Prindle, Weber, & Schmidt, 1974. Pp. 42–43.
20. Dantzig, T. *Number: the language of science* (4th Ed). New York: MacMillan, 1954. Page 6.
21. Tylor, E. B. *Primitive culture,* Vol. I (4th Ed). London: John Murray (Publisher), 1903. Pp. 241–242.
22. Churchill, E. M. *Counting and measuring.*
23. Riess, A. *An analysis of children's number responses.*
24. Schaeffer, B., Eggleton, V. H., and Scott, J. L. Number development in young children. *Cognitive Psychology,* 6 (1974): 357–379.

CHAPTER 2

1. Whitehead, A. N. *The aims of education.* New York: MacMillan, 1929. Page 7.
2. Pollack, R. H. and Brenner, M. W. (Eds). *The experimental psychology of Alfred Binet.* New York: Springer Publishing Co., 1969.
3. Bloom, L. *Language development: form and function in emerging grammars.* Cambridge, Mass. M.I.T. Press, 1970.
4. Bloom, L., Lightbown, P., and Hood, L. Structure and variation in child language. *Monographs of the Society for Research in Child Development,* 40 (1975), serial number 160.
5. Piaget, J. *The origins of intelligence in children.* New York: International Universities Press, 1952b. Page 185.
6. Mounoud, P. and Bower, T. G. R. Conservation of weight in infants. *Cognition,* 3 (1974): 29–40.
7. Piaget, J. *The origins of intelligence in children.* Page 241.
8. Papousek, H. Individual variability in learned responses in human infants. In R. J. Robinson (Ed.), *Brain and early behavior.* London: Academic Press, 1969.
9. Binet, A. The perception of lengths and numbers. In R. H. Pollack and M. W. Brenner (Eds.), *The experimental psychology of Alfred Binet.*
10. Estes, B. W. and Combs, A. Perception of quantity. *Journal of Genetic Psychology,* 108 (1966): 333–336.

11. Piaget, J. *The child's conception of number.*
12. Mermelstein, E. and Shulman, L. S. Lack of formal schooling and the acquisition of conservation. *Child Development,* 38 (1967): 39–52.
13. Opper, S. Intellectual development in Thai children. Unpublished doctoral dissertation. Cornell University, 1971.
14. Price-Williams, D. R., Gordon, W., and Ramirez, M. Skill and conservation: a study of pottery-making children. *Developmental Psychology,* 1 (1969): 769.
15. Brush, L. R. Children's conceptions of addition and subtraction: the relation of formal and informal notions. Unpublished doctoral thesis. Cornell University, 1972. Brush, L. and Ginsburg, H. Preschool children's understanding of addition and subtraction. Unpublished manuscript. Cornell University, 1971.

CHAPTER 3

1. Smith, D. E. *Numbers and numerals.* Washington: National Council of Teachers of Mathematics, 1937.
2. Smith, D. E. and Ginsburg, J. From numbers to numerals and from numerals to computation. In J. R. Newman (Ed.), *The world of mathematics,* Vol. I. New York: Simon and Schuster, 1956. Pp. 442–465.
3. Gay, J. and Cole, M. *The new mathematics and an old culture.*
4. Herndon, J. *How to survive in your native land.* New York: Bantam, 1972. Page 94.
5. Court, S. R. A. Numbers, time, and space in the first five years of a child's life. Page 82.
6. Drummond, M. *The psychology and teaching of number.* New York: World Book Company, 1922. Pp. 33–34.
7. Court, S. R. A. Numbers, time, and space in the first five years of a child's life. Page 82.
8. Court, S. R. A. Numbers, time, and space in the first five years of a child's life. Page 82.
9. Ginsburg, H. *The myth of the deprived child.* Englewood Cliffs, N.J.: Prentice-Hall, 1972.
10. McLaughlin, K. L. Number ability in preschool children. *Childhood Education,* 11 (1935): 348–353. Hebbeler, K. The development of children's problem solving skills in addition. Unpublished doctoral dissertation. Cornell University, 1976.
11. Gelman, R. How young children reason about small numbers. Paper delivered at the University of Indiana, 1975.
12. Court, S. R. A. Numbers, time, and space in the first five years of a child's life. Page 74.
13. Colburn, W. *Intellectual arithmetic upon the inductive method of instruction.* Boston: Hilliard, 1842. Page 4.

14. Hebbeler, K. The development of children's problem solving skills in addition.
15. Allardice, B. The development of written symbolism for some mathematical concepts. Unpublished doctoral dissertation. Cornell University, 1976.
16. Hebbeler, K. The development of children's problem solving skills in addition.
17. Kennedy, M. L. The case of Liam. Unpublished manuscript. Cornell University, 1976.
18. Levy, A. The case of Bob. Unpublished manuscript. Cornell University, 1976.
19. Kennedy, M. L. The case of Liam. Page 6.
20. Conant, L. L. Counting, Page 435.
21. Rosin, R. T. Gold medallions: the arithmetic calculations of an illiterate. *Council on Anthropology and Education Newsletter,* 4 (1973): 1–9.
22. Dantzig, T. *Number: the language of science.* Page 11.
23. Wall Street Journal. "Some breathing room for mankind." April 13, 1976. Page 20.
24. Dantzig, T. *Number: the language of science.* Page 3.

CHAPTER 4

1. Zaslavski, C. *Africa counts.*
2. Piaget, J. Remarks on mathematics education, *Exeter Conference on Mathematics Education,* 1972. Page 7.
3. Piaget, J. *Science of education and the psychology of the child.* New York: The Orion Press, 1970. Page 4.

CHAPTER 5

1. Erlwanger, S. H. Case studies of children's conceptions of mathematics. Unpublished doctoral dissertation. University of Illinois, 1974.
2. Dantzig, T. *Number: the language of science.* Pp. 29–30.
3. Smith, D. E. and Ginsburg, J. From numbers to numerals and from numerals to computation.
4. Allardice, B. The development of written symbolism for some mathematical concepts.
5. Cox, M. A product of our math teaching methods. Unpublished manuscript. Cornell University, 1971.
6. Behr, M., Erlwanger, S., and Nichols, E. How children view equality sentences. Unpublished paper. 1975.
7. Allardice, B. The case of Doug. Unpublished manuscript. Cornell University, 1975.

8. Houlihan, D. M. The addition methods of first and second grade children. Unpublished masters thesis. Cornell University, 1975.
9. Lankford, F. G. Some computational strategies in seventh grade pupils. Unpublished manuscript. University of Virgina, 1974.
10. Lankford, F. G. Some computational strategies in seventh grade pupils.
11. Houlihan, D. M. The addition methods of first and second grade children.
12. Petitto, A. The case of Roberta. Unpublished manuscript. Cornell University, 1975.
13. Cochran, B. S., Barson, A., and Davis, R. B. Child-created mathematics. *The Arithmetic Teacher*, 1970: 211–215.

CHAPTER 6

1. Levy, A. The case of Bob.
2. Russell, R. The case of Ralph. Unpublished manuscript. Cornell University, 1975.
3. Erlwanger, S. H. Benny's conception of rules and answers in IPI mathematics. *Journal of Children's Mathematical Behavior*, 1 (1973): 7–26, Pp. 8–9.
4. Lankford, F. G. Some computational strategies in seventh grade pupils.
5. Levy, A. The case of Bob.
6. Erlwanger, S. H. Case studies of children's conceptions of mathematics, Part I. *Journal of Children's Mathematical Behavior*, 1 (1975): 157–283. Pp. 241, 250.
7. De Jonghe, L. The case of George. Unpublished manuscript, Cornell University, 1976.
8. Erlwanger, S. H. Case studies of children's conceptions of mathematics. Page 281.
9. Freud, S. *A general introduction to psychoanalysis*. New York: Perma-books, 1960.
10. Churchill, E. M. *Counting and measuring*.
11. Davis, R. B. Personal communication. 1972.
12. McCune, N. The case of Trika. Unpublished manuscript. Cornell University, 1976.
13. Levy, A. The case of Vivian. Unpublished manuscript. Cornell University, 1975.
14. Russell, R. The case of Ralph.

CHAPTER 7

1. Levy, A. The case of Bob.
2. De Jonghe, L. The case of George.

CHAPTER 8

1. Davis, R. B. and Greenstein, R. Jennifer. *Mathematical Teachers Journal*, 19 (1964): 94–103.
2. Cox, M. A product of our math teaching methods.
3. Davis, R. B. Personal communication.
4. Fox, C. The case of Chris. Unpublished manuscript. Cornell University, 1976.
5. Court, S. R. A. Self-taught arithmetic from the age of five to the age of eight. Page 61.
6. Cohen, D. The excitement of mathematical creations. Unpublished manuscript. University of Illinois, 1975.
7. Cohen, D. The excitement of mathematical creations. Page 4.

CHAPTER 9

1. James, W. *Talks to teachers on psychology*. Pp. 7–8.
2. De Jonghe, L. The case of George. Pp. 31–32.
3. Halle, M. Literacy among the Cherokee. In J. F. Kavanagh and I. G. Mattingly (Eds.), *Language by ear and by eye*. Cambridge, Mass.: M.I.T. Press, 1972. Page 153.
4. Halle, M. Literacy among the Cherokee.
5. Hawkins, D. *The informed vision*. New York: Agathon Press, 1974. Page 29.

References

Allardice, B. The case of Doug. Unpublished manuscript. Cornell University, 1975.

Allardice, B. The development of written symbolism for some mathematical concepts. Unpublished doctoral dissertation. Cornell University, 1976.

Baldwin, B. T. and Stecher, L. I. *The psychology of the pre-school child.* New York: Appleton, D., & Co., 1925.

Behr, M., Erlwanger, S., and Nichols, E. How children view equality sentences. Unpublished paper. Florida State University, 1975.

Binet, A. The perception of lengths and numbers. In R. H. Pollack and M. W. Brenner (Eds.), *The experimental psychology of Alfred Binet.* New York: Springer Publishing Co., 1969.

Bloom, L. *Language development: form and function in emerging grammars.* Cambridge, Mass.: M.I.T. Press, 1970.

Bloom, L., Lightbown, P., and Hood, L. Structure and variation in child language. *Monographs of the Society for Research in Child Development,* 40 (1975), serial number 160.

Brush, L. R. Children's conceptions of addition and subtraction: the relation of formal and informal notions. Unpublished doctoral thesis. Cornell University, 1972.

Brush, L. and Ginsburg, H. Preschool children's understanding of addition and subtraction. Unpublished manuscript. Cornell University, 1971.

Churchill, E. M. *Counting and measuring.* Toronto: University of Toronto Press, 1961.

Cochran, B. S. Barson, A., and Davis, R. B. Child-created mathematics, *The Arithmetic Teacher,* 1970. Pp. 211–215.

Cohen, D. The excitement of mathematical creations, Unpublished manuscript. University of Illinois, 1975.

Colburn, W. *Intellectual arithmetic upon the inductive method of instruction.* Boston: Hilliard, 1842.

Conant, L. L. Counting, In J. R. Newman (Ed.), *The world of mathematics,* Vol. I. New York Simon and Schuster, 1956. Pp. 432–441.

Court, S. R. A. Numbers, time, and space in the first five years of a child's life. *Pedagogical Seminary,* 27 (1920): 71–89.

Court, S. R. A. Self-taught arithmetic from the age of five to the age of eight. *Pedogogical Seminary,* 30 (1923): 51–68.

Cox, M. A product of our math teaching methods. Unpublished manuscript. Cornell University, 1971.

Dantzig, T. *Number: the language of science* (4th Ed). New York: MacMillan, 1954.

Davis, R. B. Personal communication. 1972.

Davis, R. B. and Greenstein, R. Jennifer. *Mathematical Teachers Journal,* 19 (1964): 94–103.

De Jonghe, L. The case of George. Unpublished manuscript. Cornell University, 1976.

Drummond, M. *The psychology and teaching of number,* New York: World Book Company, 1922.

Erlwanger, S. H. Benny's conception of rules and answers in IPI mathematics. *Journal of Children's Mathematical Behavior,* 1 (1973): 7–26.

Erlwanger, S. H. Case studies of children's conceptions of mathematics. Unpublished doctoral dissertation. University of Illinois, 1974.

Erlwanger, S. H. Case studies of children's conceptions of mathematics, Part I. *Journal of Children's Mathematical Behavior,* 1 (1975): 157–283.

Estes, B. W. and Combs, A. Perception of quantity. *Journal of Genetic Psychology,* 108 (1966) 333–336.

Fox, C. The case of Chris. Unpublished manuscript. Cornell University, 1976.

Freud, S. *A general introduction to psychoanalysis.* New York: Permabooks, 1960.

Gay, J. and Cole, M. *The new mathematics and an old culture.* New York: Holt, Rinehart and Winston, 1967.

Gelman, R. How young children reason about small numbers. Paper delivered at the University of Indiana, 1975.

Gibson, E. J. and Levin, H. *The psychology of reading.* Cambridge, Mass.: MIT Press, 1975.

Ginsburg, H. *The myth of the deprived child.* Englewood Cliffs, N.J.: Prentice-Hall, 1972.

Ginsburg, H. and Opper, S. *Piaget's theory of intellectual development: an introduction.* Englewood Cliffs, N.J.: Prentice-Hall, 1969.

Grossman, A. The case of John. Unpublished manuscript. Cornell University, 1976.

Halle M. Literacy among the Cherokee. In J. F. Kavanagh and I. G. Mattingly (Eds.), *Language by ear and by eye.* Cambridge, Mass.: M.I.T. Press, 1972.

Hawkins, D. *The informed vision.* New York: Agathon Press, 1974.

Hebbeler, K. The development of children's problem solving skills in addition. Unpublished doctoral dissertation. Cornell University, 1976.

Herndon, J. *How to survive in your native land.* New York: Bantam, 1972.

Houlihan, D. M. The addition methods of first and second grade children. Unpublished masters thesis. Cornell University, 1976.

James, W. *Talks to teachers on psychology.* New York: Holt, Henry, & Co., 1939.

Kennedy, M. L. The case of Liam. Unpublished manuscript. Cornell University, 1976.

Lankford, F. G. Some computational strategies in seventh grade pupils. Unpublished manuscript. University of Virginia, 1974.

Levy, A. The case of Bob. Unpublished manuscript. Cornell University, 1976.

Levy, A. The case of Vivian. Unpublished manuscript. Cornell University, 1975.

McCune, N. The case of Trika. Unpublished manuscript. Cornell University, 1976.

McLaughlin, K. L. Number ability in preschool children. *Childhood Education,* 11 (1935): 348–53.

Mermelstein, E. and Shulman, L. S. Lack of formal schooling and the acquisition of conservation. *Child Development,* 38 (1967): 39–52.

Mounoud, P. and Bower, T. G. R. Conservation of weight in infants. *Cognition,* 3 (1974): 29–40.

Opper, S. Intellectual development in Thai children. Unpublished doctoral dissertation. Cornell University, 1971.

Papousek, H. Individual variability in learned responses in human infants. In R. J. Robinson (Ed.), *Brain and early behavior.* London: Academic Press, 1969.

Petitto, A. The case of Roberta. Unpublished manuscript. Cornell University, 1975.

Piaget, J. *The child's conception of number.* London: Routledge & Kegan Paul, 1952a.

Piaget, J. *The origins of intelligence in children.* New York: International Universities Press, 1952b.

Piaget, J. Remarks on mathematics education. Exeter Conference on Mathematics Education, 1972.

Piaget, J. *Science of education and the psychology of the child.* New York: The Orion Press 1970.

Pollack, R. H. and Brenner, M. W. (Eds.), *The experimental psychology of Alfred Binet.* New York: Springer Publishing Co., 1969.

Posner, J. K. Personal communication. 1976.

Potter, M. C. and Levy, E. J. Spatial enumeration without counting. *Child Development,* 39 (1968): 265–273.

Price-Williams, D. R., Gordon, W., and Ramirez, M. Skill and conservation: a study of pottery-making children. *Developmental Psychology,* 1 (1969): 769.

Riess, A. An analysis of children's number responses, *Harvard Educational Review*, 13 (1943): 149–162.

Renwick, E. *Children learning mathematics*. Elms Court, England: Arthur H. Stockwell 1963.

Rosin, R. T. Gold medallions: the arithmetic calculations of an illiterate. *Council on Anthropology and Education Newsletter*, 4 (1973): 1–9.

Russell, R. The case of Ralph. Unpublished manuscript. Cornell University, 1975.

Schaeffer, B., Eggleton, V. H., and Scott, J. L. Number development in young children. *Cognitive Psychology*, 6 (1974): 357–379.

Smith, D. E. *Numbers and numerals*. Washington: National Council of Teachers of Mathematics, 1937.

Smith, D. E. and Ginsburg, J. From numbers to numerals and from numerals to computation. In J. R. Newman (Ed.), *The world of mathematics*, Vol. I. New York Simon and Schuster, 1956. Pp. 442–465.

Tylor, E. B. *Primitive Culture*, Vol. 1 (4th Ed). London: John Murray (Publishers), 1903.

Wall Street Journal. "Some breathing room for mankind." April 13, 1976. Page 20.

Wertheimer, M. Numbers and numerical concepts in primitive peoples. In W. D. Ellis (Ed.), *A sourcebook of gestalt psychology*. New York: Humanities Press, 1967.

Wheeler, M. E. The untutored acquisition of writing skill. Unpublished doctoral dissertation. Cornell University, 1971.

Whitehead, A. N. *The aims of education*. New York: MacMillan, 1929.

Zaslavsky, C. *Africa counts*. Boston: Prindle, Weber, & Schmidt, 1974.

Index

Addition and subtraction
  with counting, 53–57
  without counting, 39–41
  written aids, 57–63
African mathematics. See Cross-
  cultural evidence
Algorithms, learning of, 91–92, 95–
  98
Allardice, B., 59, 82, 130, 187, 188
Arithmetic in everyday life. See
  Practical arithmetic

Baldwin, B. T., 185
Behr, M., 188
Binet, A., 33, 34, 35, 175, 186
Bloom, L., 31, 186
Bower, T. G. R., 186
Brenner, M. W., 186
Brush, L. R., 187

Calculation. See Algorithms,
  learning of; Invented
  procedures; Computation;
  Written symbolism
Churchill, E. M., 22, 25, 29, 186, 189
Cochran, B. S., 189
Cohen, D., 190
Colburn, W., 56, 187
Cole, M., 185, 187
Combs, A., 186

Computation, inconsistency in,
  116–121, 153. See also
  Algorithms; Invented
  Procedures
Conant, L. L., 63, 64, 185, 187
Concepts, mathematical
  babies, 30–33
  young children, 33–43
  See also Number words; More and
    less; Conservation; Addition
    and subtraction
Conservation, 26–28, 36–39, 40, 74
Counting. See Counting things;
  Finger counting; Invented
  procedures; Number words
Counting things, 10–20
  animals' abilities, 15
  strategies for, 15–20
Court, S. R. A., 7, 46, 47, 55, 72, 167,
  185, 187, 190
Cox, M., 188, 189
Cross-cultural evidence, 7, 18, 19,
  24, 31, 34, 40, 45, 63, 64, 65

Dantzig, T., 64, 65, 81, 186, 188
Davis, R. B., 189, 190
De Jonghe, L., 130, 174, 189, 190
Drummond, M., 7, 185

Enumeration. See Counting things

Environment, 30, 31, 45, 69, 70
Erlwanger, S. H., 111, 188, 189
Errors, 9, 68, 69, 107–129
　　nature of, 108–110, 113–116, 143,
　　175–176
　　origins of, 110–113
Estes, B. W., 186

Finger counting, 55, 56, 57, 63, 64,
　　65, 66, 72, 73, 93, 94, 132
Fox, C., 190
Freud, S., 121, 189

Gaps between written and informal
　　work, 121–129, 131, 132, 133,
　　135, 136, 179, 180, 181
Gay, J., 185, 187
Gelman, R., 23, 187
Gibson, E. J., 74
Ginsburg, H., 102, 187
Ginsburg, J., 187, 188
Greenstein, R., 189
Grossman, A., 7, 185

Halle, M., 177, 190
Hawkins, D., 190
Hebbeler, K., 187, 188
Herndon, J., 45, 46, 187
History of mathematics, 45, 81
Houlahan, D. M., 94, 188, 189

Ideas, mathematical. See Concepts
Inconsistency. See Computation,
　　inconsistency in
Instant recognition of number, 16,
　　17
Instruction. See Teaching
Interviewing, informal, 172–174
Intuition, mathematical. See
　　Concepts, mathematical
Invented procedures, 92–106, 179

James, W., 169, 185, 190

Kennedy, M. L., 61, 62, 188

Lankford, F. G., 95, 188, 189
Learning
　　Motivation for, 44–48
　　Nature of, 48–52, 176–177, 181
Learning difficulties, 130–149
Learning disabilities. See Learning
　　difficulties
Levin, H., 74
Levy, A., 130, 188, 189
Levy, E. J., 185

McCune, N., 189
McLaughlin, K. L., 187
Mermelstein, E., 187
Mistakes. See Errors
More and less, concept of, 33–35
Mounoud, P., 186

Newman, J. R., 185
New math, 73
Number words
　　learning of, 3–10
　　meaning of, 21–29
　　rote memory in, 4–5
　　underlying rules, 5–8

One-to-one correspondence, 12–15,
　　37
Opper, S., 102, 187

Papousek, H., 186
Perception of number, 160–168,
　　182–183
Petitto, A., 189
Piaget, J., 13, 29, 32, 36, 39, 40, 51,
　　69, 73, 75, 90, 98, 103, 151, 185,
　　186, 187, 188
Place value, understanding of, 85–
　　90, 91
Pollack, R. H., 186
Posner, J. K., 35, 185, 186
Potter, M. C., 185
Practical arithmetic, 52–65
Preyer, W., 31
Price-Williams, D. R., 187

Readiness, 74
Reading numbers, 83
Reiss, A., 23, 186
Renwick, E., 24, 186
Rosin, R. T., 188
Rote learning, 4–5, 72
Russell, R., 125, 189

Schaeffer, B., 186
Schooling, role of in mathematical
    thought. *See* Cross-cultural
    evidence
Shulman, L. S., 187
Smith, D. E., 187, 188
Standard tests, 121, 144, 149, 169–
    173
Stecher, L. I., 185
Subitizing. *See* Instant recognition
    of number

Symbolism. *See* Written symbolism

Teaching, 67–75, 136, 144, 149,
    169–183
Tulis, E., 49
Tylor, E. B., 186

Understanding, 150–168

Wertheimer, M., 24, 186
Wheeler, M., 49
Whitehead, A. N., 30, 186
Writing numbers, 79–82
Written symbolism, 57–63, 79–90,
    121–129, 178–179

Zaslavsky, C., 186, 188